SY

The Life & Times of Sylvia Court

An Autobiography

Copyright © 2017 Sylvia Court

All rights reserved.

ISBN-13: **978-1544839691**
ISBN-10: **1544839693**

INTRODUCTION

They say that old photographs can induce powerful memories and I know that is true. One day, feeling particularly old and decrepit, I came across a pile of faded pictures which nostalgically evoked the days of my youth; a time when I was strong and healthy and had a whole world of opportunities before me. I was just a shy girl from a normal working class background but I had a wonderful life and met some very interesting and colourful characters. I believe family history is important and should be recorded for future generations - which is the reason for this book; created while I still have the capacity to remember and the ability to write. It includes the first 22 years of my life up to my wedding in 1965, plus a few other later significant events. The next 50 + years of my marriage are fully covered in the book I wrote in my husband's memory – David: The Life & Times of David Court (which is a companion and counterpart to this one).

CONTENTS

1	Mum's Story	1
2	Dad's Story	12
3	1940 - 1949	24
4	1950 - 1954	41
5	1955 - 1959	60
6	1960 - 1965	75
7	Finding Chuck	102
8	In Conclusion	108

CHAPTER 1
MUM'S STORY

My Mum was Joyce Alice Georgina Banks (nee Mundon) (1911-2000), third daughter of Edward Henry and Sarah Ann Mundon.

We'll begin her story at the beginning of the 20th century (shortly after the death of Queen Victoria). The date was 19th October 1902. The location was St Luke's church, Holloway in the parish of Islington in London. The occasion was the wedding of Edward Henry Mundon and Sarah Ann Simpson, Mum's parents.

Edward was born in Chelsea in June 1878 and was baptised on 16th August at Holy Trinity Church in Chelsea. His father was William Mundon, (born 1854 in Farnham, Hampshire) and his mother Georgiana (born 1855 in Eye, Suffolk). He had a younger brother Charles (born 1880) who became a London cabbie. They lived above the stables in Clover Mews, London, just around the corner to the Thames Embankment & Cheyne Walk, a very wealthy and prestigious part of London. At the time of the 1901 census the family worked with the horses. William was a coachman; Edward was a footman & groom and Charles was a groom. Apparently the mews have changed very little in appearance over the last century. However, in 2005 4 Clover Mews sold for £1,800,000!

Sarah Ann Simpson was born on 4th July 1874. Unlike her husband, Edward who was born and bred in London, Sarah Ann was a country girl, growing up in the Cotswolds in the rural heart of England.

Her father was Mark Simpson, the son of Edward (born 1801) & Martha (born 1811). He was born in 1839 in Kencott, Oxfordshire and worked as a shepherd. He married his wife, Sarah, in 1856 in Witney. She was born in 1836 in Clanfield, Oxfordshire. Apparently she had an Irish grandmother & Scottish grandfather.

Sarah Ann (known as Annie) was born in Westwell, Oxfordshire and had four sisters, Jane (born 1860), Lucy (born 1862) Clara (born 1864), Louisa (born 1869) and Emily (born 1876). She also had two brothers, James (born 1866), who became a guard on the Great Western Railway and William (born 1872), who died young. There was also Alice (born 1880, granddaughter of Mark) the daughter of one of the sisters. The 1861 census lists another daughter, Amelia aged 3 but we could not find any mention of her thereafter.

At the time of the 1881 census the family was living in Badgington (Bagendon) with 10 of them living in one small stone cottage. By 1891 they had moved again to a small cottage in the nearby village of Daglingworth near Cirencester, where Mark died in 1899.

Sarah Ann Simpson married Edward Henry Mundon on 19th October 1902 at St Luke's church, Holloway in the parish of Islington in London. By 1902 the Victorian era was well and truly over and the coronation of her son, Edward VII, had taken place on 9th August.

Sarah Simpson (Sarah Ann's mother) was now a widow. Her husband Mark had died in 1899 aged 60.

Jane had married George Alfred Corpe in 1899 and was living in London at 22 Brook Road in Holloway with her son George and 3 daughters, Jane, Florence & Jessie.

Clara had also married in 1888. Her husband was William James Teal. They were living in a cottage in Daglingworth with their 3 sons, Charles, Walter & Sidney & a daughter, Lucy.

William had married Emily and was living in Maidenhead with their 3 children; a son, Charles & 2 daughters, Gladys & Stella.

James was living in Swindon where he worked as a guard for the Great Western Railway. He married Ann.

Lucy was in service with Richard & Laura Jones at Kemble in Gloucestershire.

One of the most interesting houses at which Edward and Sarah worked was Cragside House situated near Rothbury in the Borders. It was the family home of Lord Armstrong, Victorian inventor and industrialist and was described in 1880 as 'a palace of the modern magician'.

The revolutionary home of Lord Armstrong, Victorian inventor and landscape genius, was a wonder of its age. Built on a rocky crag high above Debdon Burn, the house is crammed with ingenious gadgets and was the first in the world to be lit by hydro-electricity.

Cragside has a garden of breathtaking drama, whatever the season. Lord Armstrong constructed 5 lakes, one of Europe's largest rock gardens, and planted over 7 million trees and shrubs. Today this magnificent estate can be explored on foot or by car and provides one of the last shelters for the endangered red squirrel.

Today Cragside is owned by the National Trust and has become one of the most popular places to visit in Northumberland.

Lord & Lady Armstrong also kept a house in London and their staff

would have travelled with them between the two. When they were staying at Cragside Annie & Edward lived in a cottage in the grounds. Annie was a respected cook and Edward was head footman. Lord Armstrong was one of the first people to acquire a motor car and Edward became one of the earliest chauffeurs.

Annie and Edward Mundon had four daughters;
- Gladys Kathleen Annie ("Ciss" 1904-1976) Born 02.09.1904.
- Dorothy Ivy Eleanor ("Dot" 1907-1987) Born 07.06.1907.
- Joyce Alice Georgina ("Joy" 1911-2000) Born 14.01.1911.
- Edna May Louisa ("Eddie" 1913 – 1977) Born 17.07.1913.

Picture of Annie, Edward, Gladys, Dorothy & Joyce enjoying a day on the beach at Great Yarmouth in 1912.

By the time Joyce was born in 1911 the family was living at West End Cottage in Totteridge.

Edward & Annie worked at Barnes Park (also known as Wykeham Rise) the home of Sir William Barclay Peat and his wife Edith; Edward was the butler and Annie the cook.

As well as their country estate in Totteridge, Lord and Lady Peat also kept a London residence in Eaton Square. In 1914, when Joyce was 3, the Mundon family moved to Chelsea, where they were to stay for the next 17 years. They lived on the first floor of 26, Gertrude Street. This once grand house with its impressive entrance and leafy garden had now become a place of multiple occupancy. There were three families living in the house, all sharing the same toilet and tap. Joyce had vivid recollections of the house. A very strange family, the Stringers, lived in the basement. They kept chickens and had a dog called Nigger. They had many lodgers and were often drunk.

Mrs. Long lived on the ground floor. She had the best of everything; her front room was very modern for its day with an Indian carpet and "Gay Nineties" pictures. She had a wooden bed (not the common cast iron type), a wash stand and the very best china in the kitchen. She lived alone but had a son, Ronald Long, nicknamed "Bubbles". Mrs. Long used to chat for ages with Annie. Bubbles, who was to become Joyce's best childhood friend, shared a pram with Eddie. On the first floor lived Annie, Edward and their four daughters. The family lived in very cramped conditions and the four girls had to share two single beds. There were two big windows in the front room and a cooking range sat in the marble fireplace. Rows of white canvas shoes were always lined up on the sunny kitchen windowsill. Grapevines thrived outside the window and in the garden, beyond a flower covered archway were two sycamore trees. Unfortunately the garden had become taken over by the Stringers and their chickens. The toilet, shared by everyone, contained the only tap in the house and had a stained glass window depicting a knight in armour wielding a sword.

While her friend, Bubbles, went to St Marks College, Chelsea, Joyce and her sisters attended Park Walk School near the Kings Road, which is still in existence today. Joyce did well and won a number of prizes for good work.

On Saturdays, if the weather was fine, the children would walk across the river to the nearby Battersea Park. On more inclement days they would visit the museums in South Kensington. Joyce loved going to the Natural History Museum.

Aunt Emmie (who had a son, Leslie), ensured that Joyce always had good shoes by taking her to a specialist shoe shop in Kensington called Daniel Neal & sons.

In the summer a special treat for the girls was their regular trip to the Cotswolds to stay with the Simpson relatives at Daglingworth. Granny (Sarah Simpson) lived with Aunt Lucy who had previously been a lady's maid in Maidenhead before moving back to Daglingworth.

They travelled down from London by steam train and James (Uncle Jim) would be waiting on the platform at Swindon, where he worked, with refreshments for the journey.

For children brought up in the city, this visit to the countryside was a wonderful opportunity to get to know nature at its best and really enjoy country life.

Daglingworth 1919

Summer Holidays in the Cotswolds

The girls really enjoyed their visits to the Cotswolds. The pictures of Dot & Joyce were taken in 1919. The following summer of 1920 they were joined by their younger sister, Eddie. They had fond memories of kind "Uncle Dudley" (Strickland) who was no relation but was very good to them.

Joyce was close to her father who was very kind and spiritually minded. One lovely memory she had was of a beautiful musical box, normally shut away, but which he occasionally brought out to entertain the children as a special treat. Although, at the time she did not understand the relevance of it, she particularly treasured one book he gave her - "The scenario of the Photo-drama of Creation".

In 1921, when Joyce was 10, Edward was working as a chauffeur in Eaton Square. He drove a state-of-the-art Minerva Limousine. His brother, Charles, was working as a London cabbie. Edward had spent long winter evenings studying "the Knowledge" and he, too, was about to embark on a new career as a taxi driver. One day when attempting to start the engine of the limousine the starting handle kicked back, as it often did, and grazed his hand. Unfortunately this small scratch became infected and, without the antibiotics we have today, he soon became fatally ill with septicaemia (blood poisoning) and died just a few days later. Edward was young and healthy and had never had a day's illness in his life so his tragic death came as a terrible shock. Annie was distraught and the family was devastated. Her bereavement left Annie so traumatised that Joyce was sent away to live with her rich Aunt Alice.

Aunt Alice (1880-1974) was actually Joyce's cousin, the daughter of one of her aunts. Like the others she left home to go into service and in 1911 was working as a barmaid in London. By 1918 she had changed her name to Alys Maude and married into the aristocracy. Her husband was Francis Edward Gage (1860-1936), twenty years her senior, the son of Lt.-Gen. Hon. Edward Thomas Gage and Arabella Elizabeth Gage

Francis Gage was educated at Wellington College, Berkshire, England. He was an immigration officer at Tyne Port, England and lived in a large country house at Rowlands Gill near Newcastle.

Almost immediately after her father's sudden death, Joyce was sent up North to live with Aunt Alice at her large country house in the Derwent Valley. She stayed at Rowlands Gill for about 6 months, returning to London in January 1922. Despite the beautiful scenery and a rope swing across the river it was not a happy time for her.

Alice, despite her wealth, was very mean. She insisted that Joyce draw out her own life savings in order to buy a new coat to replace her old worn one which Alice considered to be too shabby. A young Indian girl lived at the house, but she too was also treated badly. Husband Francis (known as Frank) did not fare much better. He was banished to the attic where he played the violin while Alice, apparently, spent much of her time with a Mr. Bain.

An interesting piece of family history relates to the greengage (Prunus domestica italica or the Reine Claude) a cultivar of the plum. Sources attribute the origin of the name Greengage to several members of the Gage family. One account states that the cultivar was brought into England by the Rev. John Gage who obtained them from the Chartreuse Monastery. "Green Gages" were imported into England from France in 1724 by Sir William Gage, 7th Baronet, from whom they get their English name.

Francis died in 1936 and rumour has it that the cause of death was that he sat on his shooting stick the wrong way up, but that cannot be verified!

Alice married again in 1942. She married Ernest Saveall in St Austell, Cornwall. He died in 1971 and Alice died in Falmouth in 1974 aged 94.

Joyce left Rowlands Gill and returned to London In January 1922 but her mother, the recently widowed Annie, was experiencing a very difficult time. Not only did she have to support the family but she also had to cope single-handedly with four young and attractive daughters.

When Ciss left school she began working at a florist shop in Fulham Road. Her main duty was making wreaths for funerals. Unfortunately she had an aversion to maggots and since these were often found in the sphagnum moss that was an essential component in the construction of wreaths, her career as a florist was rather short lived!

She was obviously artistic and managed to get taken on as an apprentice milliner at Maud Moore's, an exclusive and very expensive hat shop in Kensington, opposite Harrods. Ciss was attractive and popular and soon became part of the London social scene which included such well known and controversial characters as the Mitford girls.

Ciss's hectic social life was a constant source of anxiety to Annie who, concerned about her late nights, used to lie in wait with a broom to teach her a lesson when she eventually returned!

Ciss had many men friends but her first serious boyfriend was Ron Playford probably because he had a motorbike. They often went out biking together – until the novelty wore off! She left him for a much older man, Walter White, at least ten years her senior. Walter had been in the Navy in the First World War serving on HMS Agamemnon. He was involved in the ferocious Battle of Jutland in 1916 where he lost a leg when his ship was sunk. He was a good singer and Ciss accompanied him on the piano. He worked in the sorting office at the Post Office and used to follow Ciss's bus on his bike! When she eventually tired of him she went out with Billy Christie, a sergeant in the Territorial Army. She married Bill in 1929 and they had one daughter Pamela, born in 1933. Ciss died in 1976.

Dot's first job was as a nursery maid, living out. It was very hard work, scrubbing floors and carrying coals. Concerned about her health her doctor, Doctor Mansell from the Cromwell Road, offered her a job. Finally she found the job she really loved – as a nursemaid to Helena Lambton Helena was the daughter of Arthur Lambton, a cousin of the Earl of Durham. He lived at 32 Argyll Mansions, Kings Road, Chelsea and was quite a colourful character - a well-known London sportsman and man-about-town.

Arthur Lambton was a friend of Conan Doyle and founded the "Crimes Club" in London. He was particularly interested in the Jack the Ripper murders and wrote much on this subject. He was a highly respected author and wrote many newspaper articles. At the time, the Lambton family was one of the oldest and richest families in England.

Dot worked for the Lambtons up until the time she married Alfred Whiffen in 1931. Helena was very fond of her former nurse and kept in touch with Dot throughout her life. Dot and Alf's daughter, Gillian was born in 1943 and Dot died in 1987.

Joyce did well at Park Walk School but, for financial reasons, had to leave before she was 14.

Her first job was in Radcliffe Gardens as a mother's help to a rather naughty little boy. After just a few weeks, she went down with influenza and had to leave. She then worked at a large house in Pullens Square, near South Kensington doing cleaning and kitchen work.

There was a lot of backbiting going on between the cook and the housemaid - and the scullery boy, who obviously fancied her, carved their initials under the draining board!

Joyce eventually managed to get a job with Ciss at Maud Moore's exclusive millinery shop but she had to work very long hours in an underground room for seven shillings and sixpence a week (37p). However, she worked her way steadily up through the business, first becoming an improver (matching up ribbons and dying felt) and then a copyist. She transferred from Maud Moore's in Knightsbridge to their Bond Street branch and then, as a fully qualified milliner, to South Croydon when her boss Miss Rose opened up her own hat shop there. She then moved to a very exclusive Jewish millinery shop in Wellesley Road and then finally to one in George Street, Croydon.

1920's

Annie, Joyce and Eddie continued to live in Gertrude Street until the early 30's when Annie managed to buy 73, Priory Crescent, a brand new house in Cheam for the princely sum of £750. This same house was sold in 2006 for £300,000 – a 40,000% rise! Dot and Alf, who shared the purchase cost, lived on the first floor while Annie, Joyce and Eddie had the downstairs flat. Annie was to share this house with Dot and her family for her remaining 44 years. She died of cancer in 1956.

In 1931 something happened that caused a lot of regret and anguish in the family and would affect Joyce for the rest of her life – but more about that in another chapter.

Holidays with Eddie

Late 1930's

In 1939, Joyce and Eddie went on holiday together to Jersey in the Channel Islands where she met Jimmy Pearce (real name James Banks), a professional boxer, who lived in West Croydon. Her first impression of him was that he was rather too skinny. She soon realised that you cannot judge a book by its cover. They married in June the following year.

CHAPTER 2
DAD'S STORY
A MYSTERY UNRAVELLED

My Dad was James Banks, known as Jim (1914-1978). From an early age I had been puzzled by the fact that Dad's surname was 'Banks' but his parents were called 'Pearce'. However it seemed to be a very sensitive subject and something that was never discussed in our home during his lifetime. Mysteries intrigue me and I was determined to find the truth.

We know that on the 8th June 1940, a wedding took place at St. Dustan's Church, Cheam Surrey. The bride, dressed in a beautiful home-made gown of parachute silk, was Joyce Mundon – my Mum. According to this newspaper cutting, the bridegroom was Mr Jimmy Pearce, the well-known Croydon boxer.

However, the marriage certificate gives the bridegroom's name as James Banks, son (apparently) of William Alfred Banks, labourer (dec'd.). This raises a very intriguing question. Who was James Banks and why had he been widely known as Jimmy Pearce?

We found another newspaper cutting which sheds a little more light on the mystery by informing us that Jimmy Pearce was adopted and that his real name was James Banks. This must have come as a surprise to the people of Croydon. They had known him, not only as a talented boxer but also as a bit of an entrepreneur with his horse and cart, working as a high class fruiterer and greengrocer, potato merchant and removals man – in fact the "man with a van" of his time!

The only real clue we have to his identity is a copy of his birth certificate. (During his lifetime I never saw his birth certificate although I was recently able to send off for a copy). This gives us three irrefutable facts – the date of his birth, the place of his birth and the name, residence and occupation of his natural mother.

The Date – James Banks was born on September 3rd 1914.

The Place - According to his birth certificate James Banks was born at 76 Eridge Road, Thornton Heath. That address is no longer in existence as it was changed to 39 Woodcroft Road in November 1939. However 76 Eridge Road was a significant and rather notorious address. It was actually a euphemism for the Croydon Union Workhouse which means that around the time of his birth, James' mother was actually living in the workhouse.
(It is an interesting fact that after 1904 a birth certificate was not legally permitted to state that a birth took place in a workhouse. Instead the postal address of the workhouse was given as the place of birth).

The Birth Mother - On the birth certificate the name of the mother was given as Agnes Banks. Agnes was born in Beddington (a country village on the outskirts of Croydon) in September 1888, the youngest of four children.

Once we could confirm the identity of his biological mother we were able to discover her history.

Her parents were Ann (born in Chelsea in 1853) and Henry Banks (born in Mitchum in 1850). She had two older sisters, Sarah Ann (born in 1880), and Matilda (born in 1883). She also had a brother, Henry (born in 1885).

Her grandparents on her father's side were Thomas Banks (born in 1815, son of Thomas Banks (born in 1784) who farmed 15 acres in Little Horsted, Sussex) and Matilda (born in Brighton in 1816). After their marriage they lived at the top of Mitchum Causeway where Thomas worked as a "Carman". (A Carman was a driver of horse-drawn vehicles for transporting goods. Carmen were often employed by railway companies for local deliveries and collections of goods and parcels. It was the modern day equivalent of a van driver).

Henry (Agnes' father) was one of ten children, the others being William, Thomas, Marion, Mary Ann, Eliza, Elizabeth, James, Ellen & Harriet (Agnes's uncles and aunts).

In 1901 Agnes (then aged 12 was living with her family at the Nursery, Beddington which was being farmed by her father Henry and brother Henry Jnr.

By 1911 (ten years later) Agnes (by then working as a domestic servant) was boarding at the home of her eldest sister, Sarah, who was married to George Towers, a railway guard. They lived at 165 Dennett Road, Croydon with their four children, George, Annie, Lily and Violet. Her father (then aged 62 and widowed) was still a farmer and was living at what was then known as Banks Farm, Beddington with a new "wife" 37 year old Ada Julia Banks (although we could find no record of a marriage).

In 1914 Agnes was pregnant and (like many unmarried mothers) was living in the Union Workhouse. According to the workhouse records an entry for an Agnes Banks, born 1888, appears in Admission & Discharge Registers of the workhouse. She was admitted to the Croydon Union Workhouse on 25 June 1914 and discharged on 19 August 1914 (probably to live in at Holmedale Cottage, Addington Lane, Mitcham Road, Croydon, where she was assigned to work as a domestic help under the workhouse jurisdiction).

Under the heading 'Name and Address of Friends' the workhouse record reads; *'Bro Henry Banks 21 Priory Road Croydon'*

There is an entry dated 17 September 1914 for a baby named James born to a single woman named Agnes Banks in the Infirmary Baptismal Register where most of the entries are for the babies of single women.

Croydon Workhouse, circa 1866

The workhouse was administered by the Board of Guardians and very often individuals/inmates were named in the minutes of their meetings. There is an entry for an Agnes Banks aged 26 in the minutes of the Settlement and Removal Committee 21 July 1914. Along with others she is listed under *'new bastardy cases'* which have become chargeable to the union. Although the entry in the admission register tells us she was discharged in August she is mentioned again at the following meeting 8 September 1914 which states;
'That in the case of the women Banks further enquiries are necessary.

The committee directed that proceedings be authorised against the putative father of this women's child, subject to the necessary corroborative evidence being obtainable'

This seems to have been standard practice and could be because, although not an inmate at this time, she may have been receiving assistance from the union through 'out-relief'.

She obviously was admitted back to the workhouse infirmary for the birth. She gave up her baby for adoption soon after the birth and the following year, 1915, she married Albert Veal.

We have no information about James's father. He is not recorded on the birth certificate although, curiously, a father is listed on James Banks' marriage certificate (although this is probably fictitious). Apparently it was not unusual for people whose father was unknown to fabricate a name on a marriage certificate, usually with their mother's maiden name (and hence their own surname), in order to hide the fact of their own illegitimacy. Of course there is always the remote possibility that a William Alfred Banks was the father although it is probably much more likely that the first names of his adoptive father were used in this instance.

Why did Agnes choose to name her baby James? We cannot be sure but she did have an Uncle James who was married to Sarah and had a daughter Mary who married Edward Smith in 1894. Uncle James died young in June 1998, when Agnes was 9 years old.

Adoption

No official adoptions took place before 1927 so James' adoption would have been an informal arrangement with no civil records existing. Informal adoptions would usually be arranged between family, friends and acquaintances but sometimes the babies were advertised in the newspapers.

James was adopted by a young couple, William Alfred Pearce (born in June 1889) and Clara Frances Pearce (born 27th January 1890). They had been married three years previously in 1911 and had no children.

It is possible that the Pearce family might have been related to the Banks family although we could find no evidence of this. However they certainly lived in close proximity to each other in West Croydon.

William Pearce was the son of Samuel (born 1857) and Elizabeth (born 1862) Pearce who had nine children born alive but only five of which survived. William Alfred was the oldest, followed by Alfred J (born 1893), Louisa J (born 1896), George H (born 1900) and Alice E (born 1906). They were all born locally in Croydon where Samuel worked as a corporation labourer. In 1911 the family was living at 1 Dennett Road (the same road in which Agnes was living in at that time).

Clara Frances Howard was the daughter of Henry William Howard (born 1862) and Mary Ann Howard (born 1868). They had seven children born alive, six of which survived; Ada (born 1888), Clara (born 1890), Henry (born 1892), Daisy (born 1894), Bertie (born 1897) and Edward (born 1900). Henry Howard was a wood chopper and firewood seller and the family lived at 14 Grace Street, Croydon.

Clara Howard was a bottle washer in a brewery at the time of her marriage although later she worked as a cleaner in Grants (a large Croydon department store). William Pearce was a corporation worker (a dustman) - a profession he enjoyed throughout his working life. Whenever possible, Clara would walk down to the corporation depot, past the huge steaming cooling towers of the power station, to meet him after work.

The Great War

The time shortly after James' adoption must have been very difficult for Clara. When he was 6 months old, James was taken very ill with a bad case of measles. He survived the illness but his lungs were permanently damaged and he suffered with chronic chest infections for the rest of his life.

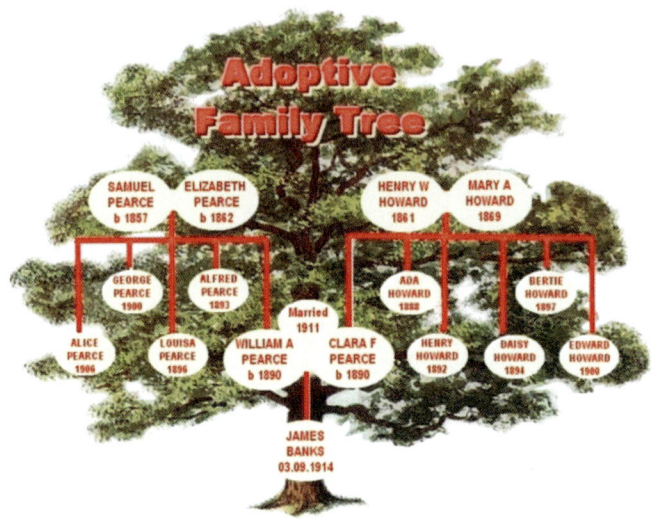

The war, which began shortly before James's birth, rapidly escalated. For the first time, Croydon experienced rationing, blackouts, air raids and compulsory military service.

Croydon was bombed by zeppelins in October 1915, and was subjected to further raids in 1916.

William and his brother, Alfred Pearce, were recruited into the Army Service Corps. They served in Egypt looking after the horses that pulled the gun carriages. The Army Service Corps were the unsung heroes of the British army in the Great War. They were the men who operated the transport. Soldiers cannot fight without food, equipment and ammunition. In the Great War, the vast majority of this tonnage, supplying a vast army on many fronts, was supplied from England. Using horses and motor vehicles, railways and waterways, the ASC performed prodigious feats of logistics and were one of the great strengths of organisation by which the war was won.

Although more than 2500 Croydon men were killed on active service in that war William came home safely (albeit with tattoos on his arms and a counterfeit ivory camel which took pride of place on the sideboard in the parlour) and life returned to normal.

SYLVIA COURT

Growing up in Lambeth Road, West Croydon.

William and Clara rented a small two up, two down, brick built terrace house in Lambeth Road West Croydon. The front door opened directly into the cosy front room which was only used for special occasions. There were lace curtains at the window where an aspidistra had pride of place. Delicate Japanese bone china tea and coffee sets (wedding presents that were never used) were displayed in glass fronted cabinets flanking the cast iron fireplace. A large heavy wooden sideboard filled most of the wall opposite the window. A heavy fringed velvet curtain separated the two downstairs rooms which were divided by the steep narrow staircase. The family spent most of their time in the back room which was much brighter and lighter. This room had a central table and armchairs either side of the fireplace. A small scullery led off this room with a butler sink and the only tap in the house. Upstairs there were two bedrooms. There was no bathroom and the toilet was outside. Tin baths hung on the wall of the yard. The garden was long and narrow and very fertile, no doubt due to the abundance of horse manure at the time. William and Clara grew a profusion of fruit and vegetables and flowers for cutting. In the summer it was a colourful sight with a wealth of gladioli, dahlias and chrysanthemums. There were wooden outbuildings at the end of the garden where rabbits, chickens and pigeons were kept. The family also had various pets as can be seen from the photographs.

William and Clara lived at 3 Lambeth Road for all their married life and it remained virtually unchanged until they both died in 1969. It was originally a rented house but the landlord mysteriously disappeared in the 1950's. After they died it went to one of Clara's nieces and was recently sold (2009) for £145,000.

James attended Rectory Manor School Croydon.

When he was eleven he won a prize for progress although he did not enjoy going to school and avoided it as much as possible. He left at the first opportunity without any qualifications and was barely literate. Many years

later he realized that he his education was sadly lacking and he attended evening classes to learn the basics on which he had originally missed out.

James had an aggressive streak which fortunately was channelled into an interest in boxing. Tom Fisher, who ran a nearby gym, recognized that he had great potential and encouraged him to

take up boxing professionally. He soon became well known as 'Jim Pearce - The Croydon Express'. Between 1937 and 1939 he boxed at welterweight and middleweight and took part in at least 14 professional contests. Probably his greatest triumph was beating the South African middleweight and lightweight champion, Eddie Pierce, at Worthing in 1937.

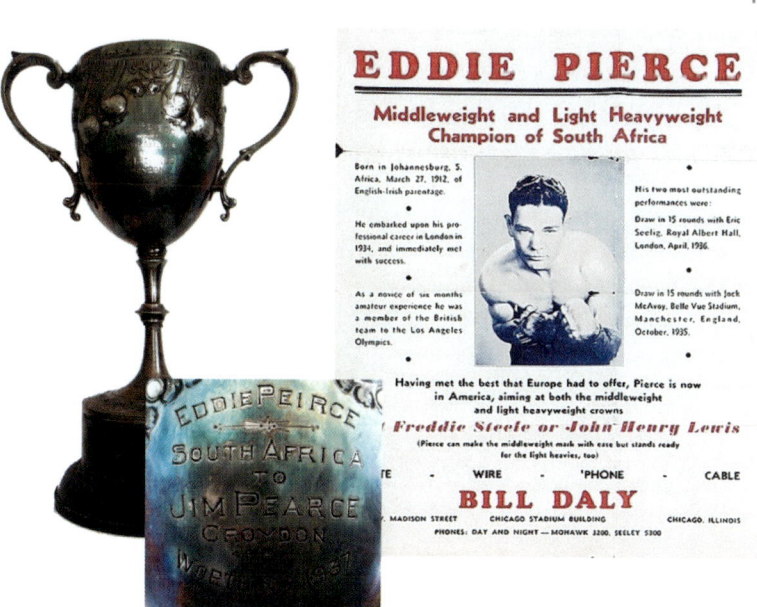

Apart from his professional boxing career James turned his hand to practically anything that did not require academic knowledge. After leaving school he worked as an errand boy and eventually started his own business with his trusty horse and cart. He did whatever work was available; removals, coal and potato deliveries and in due course ran his own greengrocery business. In 1935 he worked in a fresh fish shop and in 1940 worked as a platelayer for British Railways.

In 1939 James went on holiday to Jersey in the Channel Islands. While he was there he met Joyce Mundon who was also on holiday with her sister Eddie. They continued to see each other on their return; romance blossomed and they were married on 8th June the following year. From that moment on Jimmy Pearce, the famous Croydon boxer, reverted to his original name, James Banks, the name with which he was born.

CHAPTER 3
1940 - 1949

On Saturday the 8th of June 1940 a wedding took place at St Dunstan's Church, Cheam, Surrey. Joyce Alice Georgina Mundon of 73, Priory Crescent, Cheam was married to James Banks of 3 Lambeth Road, Croydon.

James was better known by his professional name, Jimmy Pearce. He was a well-known West Croydon boxer who earned for himself the soubriquet of 'The Croydon Express'. Opponents he had beaten include Taffy Smith, Tom Davies, Charlie Campbell,

Johnny Hughes, Gunner Edgeworth, Harry Farr, Charlie Mumford, Billy Wallace and Eddie Peirce (the South African champion). He was still under contract with Mr. Tom Fisher, the West Croydon manager but owing to his work on the Southern Railway he found little time for training. He had boxed in all the leading London halls and in nearly every town on the South Coast. After retiring from boxing he intended to open a club for boys in the Sutton district.

Joyce was a milliner and lived with her mother and sister Edna in a house they shared with her married sister, Dorothy and her husband, Alf. She wore a dress of white satin with a tulle veil and carried a bouquet of white carnations. She was given away by Mr. Fred Ockelford, a friend of the family. She had two bridesmaids; her sister Edna and her niece Pamela, daughter of her other sister, Gladys. They wore dresses of turquoise taffeta with flowered headdresses matching their bouquets of pink carnations. Mr. Walter Smith was best man. Nearly fifty guests attended the reception which was held at the bride's mother's house in Priory Crescent.

After the wedding they lived at 182 Maldon Road, Cheam, just around the corner from Joyce's previous home in Priory Crescent. It was a recently built (1930's) house which had been converted into two flats. Jim and Joyce had the ground floor flat. As can be seen from the modern photograph it has changed little over the past seven decades. It was sold in 2007 for £288,000.

Although he had worked at various occupations in the past, ranging from professional boxing, removals, deliveries, greengrocery and fishmongery, Jim was working for British Railways (Southern Region) at the time of his marriage.

He was employed as a platelayer. Platelayers worked in a gang of perhaps 8 or so men under the leadership of a ganger, looking after a certain 'length' of line. (The term dates back to the earliest days of the railways when they were known as plateways and were built using short sections of iron bar or angle sections, rather than the rails we know today). A platelayer would be responsible for all aspects of track maintenance such as replacing worn out rails or rotten sleepers, packing to ensure a level track, weeding and clearance of the drains etc. They would walk the length of their track with a long shafted hammer looking for any sort of damage. The hammer was for replacing the small blocks of wood that held the rail to the chair. Each sleeper had chairs bolted to it. The rail sat in the chair and was held by the

block of wood. (These were later replaced by metal). Platelayers were very poorly paid, but very conscientious. They were the backbone of the railways as, without decent track, they could not operate. They had little available to them in the way of mechanical assistance in those days and their work was arduous and uncomfortable.

At the outbreak of war, the National Service (Armed Forces) Act made all men between 18 and 41 liable for conscription into the armed forces. However, in 1938 a Schedule of Reserved Occupations had been drawn up, exempting certain key skilled workers from conscription. The government was determined not to repeat the mistakes of World War One, when the indiscriminate recruitment of too many men into the military had left major war production schemes short of the necessary workforce. All railway workers, together with dockworkers, miners, farmers, agricultural workers, schoolteachers and doctors were in reserved occupations. Their occupations were often far from a soft option. Hours were long and conditions often difficult, and some places of work, such as railways, factories and dockyards, were prime targets for enemy bombing. Some men in reserved occupations felt frustration at not being allowed to go and fight, while those in the armed forces envied them for not being conscripted. Many in reserved occupations joined civil defence units such as the Home Guard, the SFP or the ARP, which created additional responsibilities on top of their work.

Jim, as a railway worker, was in a reserved occupation but he also volunteered for the Home Guard (Dad's Army) doing fire watching duties at Cheam Station. This meant that, although he was working all day in his normal job, he also spent many long cold nights on a high roof watching out for fires caused by incendiary bombs dropped by the Luftwaffe. He would have worn a tin hat, an armband and carried a gun. He joked that if the Germans dropped any bombs he would catch them and throw them right back! He received the Defence Medal for three years of service.

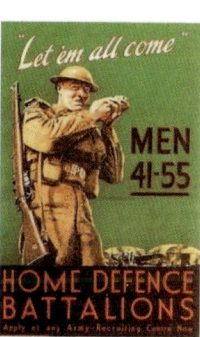

The long hours of working outside in all weathers eventually took their toll. Within just a year or so of the wedding Jim became seriously ill. What started as a mild respiratory infection progressed into bronchitis and then pneumonia. Jim had suffered with lung infections since having measles as a young baby. As a platelayer he often had to work in railway tunnels filled with toxic smoke from the steam trains. No doubt he had encountered many chest injuries during his boxing career. All these factors probably exacerbated his condition.

He developed life threatening complications and the only possible hope for survival would be radical surgery to remove

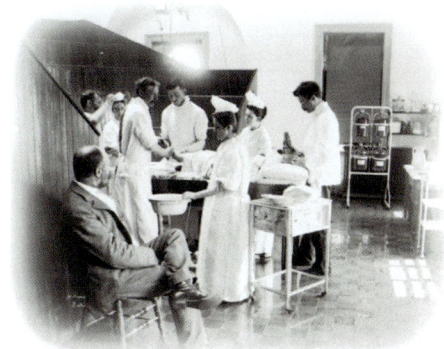

large sections of the diseased lung tissue. Unfortunately in the 1940's this procedure was virtually unknown. Since it was a matter of life or death they went ahead with what was then considered to be pioneering surgery despite the fact that the outcome seemed hopeless. Despite everyone's fears Jim did survive the operation and went down in medical history. (Many years later our family doctor, Dr. Griffin, recalled how, as a young medical student, he had been working at that hospital at the time and been deeply impressed by the success of Jim's operation).

Although Penicillin was discovered by Alexander Fleming in 1928, it was not made available for general use as an antibiotic until 1941 - which was very timely for Jim! Even so, it took many weeks of convalescing in Epsom Hospital before he was well enough to return home.

On Saturday March 13 terrible events were unfolding in Europe. German forces had liquidated the Jewish ghetto in Krakow, Hans Finke and 963 prisoners had arrived in Auschwitz; 473 people were put to death in the gas chambers and 491 were assigned to slave labor.

That was the day that I, Sylvia Dorothy Banks, came into this world. I was born at 73 Priory Crescent, Cheam Surrey, the home that Joyce had shared with her mother and sisters before her wedding. Her sister, Edna, who was still living at home, had to give up her bed in the middle of the night for the birth!

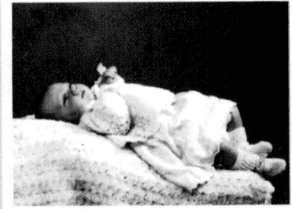

1943

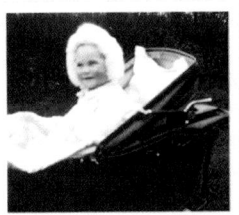

Burford Oxfordshire
on a visit to relatives in
the summer of 1943

On the 13th June 1944 at 6.25am Germany launched her Vengeance Weapons on the heart of London. Firstly came the V-1 weapons and later the terrifyingly advanced V-2 rocket. The main purpose of the V-Weapons was to terrorise the British civilian population so that the war against Germany would not continue. This failed completely with the weapons not being used until Germany had effectively lost the war. However this was the reason that over a million women, children, elderly and disabled people evacuated from the capital

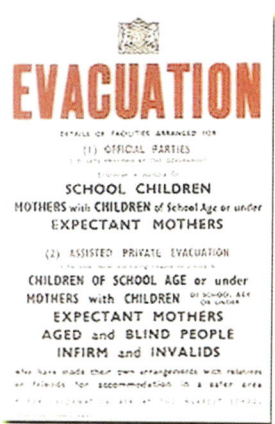

With Mr. Whitman at his cottage in Driffield, Gloucestershire in 1944.

Dad was still recovering from his operation; Mum was a new mother with me – a baby just over a year old, so it was far safer for the family to leave Cheam and evacuate to the countryside. We were billeted with a kind gentleman called Mr. Whitman. He lived in a traditional Cotswold stone cottage in the little village of Driffield near Cirencester in Gloucestershire, only a few miles away from Daglinworth where Mum spent her idyllic summer holidays as a child.

While we were away, the woman who was the tenant of the upstairs flat, Mrs. Laponse, had managed to acquire the freehold of the whole house and wanted to gain full occupancy. Although, as sitting tenants, Mum and Dad had the right to remain in the property, Mrs. Laponse embarked on a malicious campaign to drive them out.

World War Two had been the deadliest conflict in history. Well over 60 million people were killed throughout the world. In the UK alone 383,600 were killed in military service and 67,100 civilians died as a direct result of the war. Many major English cities were heavily bombed, not for military purposes but to lower morale. Food was rationed, air raid shelters were erected and heavy black-out curtains were used so the German bombers could not identify the major cities from the air. It was a very difficult and frightening time. Eventually, to everyone's relief, the war ended with Victory in Europe on 8th May 1945 and victory over Japan two months later on 15 August 1945. This marked the end of all hostilities and numerous celebratory events took place all over the country. During this time Mum was pregnant with Marilyn and I stayed with Granny and Granddad in Croydon for several weeks. A street party was held outside their house and, even though I was only two, I remember it well.

Granny and Granddad were very kind and very generous and gave me a pure white fluffy kitten – a live one - which, unfortunately I wasn't allowed to bring home with me! I was also a bridesmaid at a wedding. I can't remember the wedding itself or even who was getting married, I just remember travelling to the church in a large black car, clutching a bunch of flowers – a sweet smelling little posy of lilies-of-the-valley surrounded by maidenhair fern.

I must have stayed in Croydon for most of the summer in 1945 because when I returned home I had a new baby sister. Marilyn Joy Banks had been born on the 24th July 1945. It must have been a very difficult time for the family because of the antagonistic attitude of Mrs. Laponse, who had now become the landlady from hell. Joyce spent most of her time away from the house, taking the children to the park or to visit Auntie Dot and her daughter, Gillian, who was 9 months younger than me. I have few memories of the house in Maldon Road although I do remember Mum leaving the rent money on the post at the bottom of the stairs (obviously to avoid contact with the landlady!) I also remember sitting in the push chair and picking some beautiful sweet smelling blossom spilling out over a garden fence on the way to Auntie Dot's house. However my most vivid memory of the time was the incident of the "blue man". This occurred soon after Marilyn's birth. I was in the garden, the back door was open and Mum was bathing Marilyn in the kitchen sink. I looked up and saw a plump, iridescent blue man floating in the sky. Everyone told me it was probably some sort of barrage balloon - although to me it was definitely my 'blue man' and nothing would convince me otherwise!

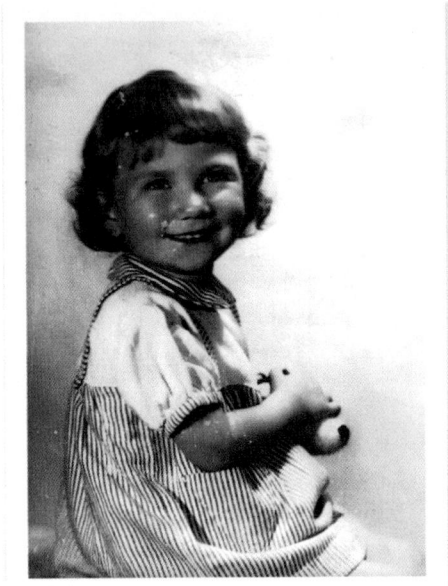

Cheam 1946

Bognor Regis
1946

Chessington Zoo with Granny &
Nonsuch Park Cheam
1947

Mum and Dad always dreamt of living in a pretty little cottage in the country which they intended to call 'Rose Cottage'. However, when the situation at the house in Cheam became intolerable they did actually move to a cottage in the country – but it was hardly a dream cottage. No.1 Pouces Cottages was the end one of an isolated terrace of small Victorian cottages on the perimeter of Manston airfield, near Minster in Thanet, Kent. It was situated in Margate Road which is now known as Spitfire Way, with fields of cabbages behind and the airfield in front.

One advantage of relocating to Thanet was to escape the unpleasantness from the former landlady. It was also very nice to move to a quiet rural area with an open outlook and surrounded by farmland. However there were major disadvantages. For example the putrid smell of rotting cabbages often hung over the green fields! The nearest towns were Ramsgate and Margate, several miles away. The closest village was Minster but to get there meant taking a short cut through the airfield and risking life and limb by crossing the runway. To get to work Dad had to cycle to Margate station and then take the slow 6.40 train to London. He left home at about 5am and returned after 9pm. This meant that the only time he had with the children was at weekends, by which time he was totally exhausted. He had to do this in all weathers, cycling through blizzard conditions and heat waves.

Unlike the house in Cheam, which was comparatively new with modern facilities, the cottage was very basic. There was neither electricity nor any insulation, so the house was bitterly cold in the winter and unbearably hot in the summer. The North wind howled around the building, rattling through the sash windows. Even our fleecy 'liberty bodices' couldn't keep out the droughts. The amenities were primitive - paraffin lamps, coal fires and tin baths. It was very difficult to keep warm in winter but in the summer the bedrooms were sometimes so hot that the only way to cool down was with wet flannels. The winter of 1947 was one of the coldest on record whereas the summer of 1949 was one of the hottest! It's no wonder we suffered with such extremes of temperature!

Soon after moving to Manston I was forced to go to school.
I say 'forced' because I really hated it and used every opportunity to pretend to be ill and stay at home. The problem was that the nearest school was situated in Ramsgate, a long bus ride away. It was not easy for a five year old to travel alone on a bus, especially when my younger sister could stay at

home with Mum! There were usually tears and tantrums when it was time to say goodbye. After school they would come down to the bus stop to meet me. Marilyn would either be asleep in the push chair or pedalling away in her little red racing car! I always thought my teacher's name was "Miss Door Snail" but Mum didn't believe me and was always embarrassed when she needed to write letters to the school! I never found out what she was really called.

The school was Dame Janet Infant School in Newington Road. It was built in 1933 on land provided by the school's benefactress Dame Janet Stancomb-Wills. Dame Janet Stancomb-Wills was born in 1853. In 1923 Dame Janet became the first woman to be awarded mayorship of Ramsgate. She had many interests, including art and architecture, but was particularly keen on raising awareness on many social and educational issues. With education being at the heart of Dame Janet's work she supported wishes for a new primary and secondary school to be built for the community of Ramsgate. Dame Janet was so committed to this project she even bought a large area of land for the new schools to be built upon. Sadly, Dame Janet died before any of the schools were built. But in 1933 her dream came true with the opening of Dame Janet School. Ramsgate had a brand new primary school to serve the community and there was no better way to thank Dame Janet than by proudly honouring her name to the school.

Our cottage in Manston couldn't have been a very healthy place to live. During the few years we lived there, Marilyn suffered from frequent bouts of tonsillitis and eventually had her tonsils removed. She vividly remembers being driven to the hospital in the car of one of our lady neighbours and looking back through the tiny oval window!

I managed to contract all the usual childhood illnesses and had measles and chicken pox at the same time. The dreaded school board man became a frequent visitor. One of Marilyn's earliest and proudest memories is of one of those many visits when he came round to find out why I was not at school. He was an ominous figure, dressed from head to toe in black, standing in the front door which opened directly into the living room. He listened to Marilyn chattering away to herself then turned to Mum and complimented her on having such a wonderfully clever daughter who could talk in perfect 'Double Dutch'. Marilyn felt very pleased with herself as she had not realised she could speak in a foreign language!

We lived on the edge of Manston airfield which, after the war ended, continued as a busy RAF base. Because our house overlooked the airfield it played a significant part in our lives. Our favourite toys were model planes - but the only ones available at the time were made of lead and not designed to fly. We discovered this with unfortunate consequences when one of the planes I was 'flying' hit Marilyn in the forehead just narrowly missing her eye.

There were also some traumatic events associated with living in such close proximity to the airfield. The nearest shop and doctor's surgery were situated in Minster - just a short distance away as the crow flies, but much further if you take the roads around the airfield. Mum normally took the short cut which involved crossing the runway. On one occasion she was taking Marilyn to the doctor's when suddenly, as they were half way across the very wide runway, they were aware of a jet roaring towards them. They threw themselves on the ground and the plane just managed to take off, skimming their heads and scorching their hair and eyebrows!

Another memorable and frightening occasion was when I was 5 and had been left alone in the house while suffering from chickenpox. It was the 18th September 1948 and a battle of Britain air display was being held at the airfield. I was disappointed that I had to stay in bed and wasn't able to be part of the excited crowds watching beside the runway. However I did watch through the bedroom window and was horrified when one of the planes (a mosquito) went out of control and appeared to be heading straight for the house. It missed the house but crashed into a car park just a short distance away, with tragic results. Apparently the pilot, whose  wife saw the accident, had led a flight of three aircraft in high-speed formation flying before breaking away to give an exhibition of aerobatics. He had twice dived at over 400 m.p.h. and then roared past the public enclosure. Gaining height he began a slow roll from which he did not pull out. The machine crashed on a road crowded with people and cars. The petrol tanks exploded and burning debris was scattered in all directions, setting fire to several cars. The intense heat hampered the work of rescuers and three victims were burnt to death in one car. Twelve people died and many more were in hospital with multiple burns.

Just a few months later I watched another incident when a spitfire was circling the house with its engine in flames, but fortunately that one made a successful emergency landing.

Apparently those two events inspired the plot of 'Trapped in the Sky', (which featured the 'Fire Flash' airliner) one of the well-known 'Thunderbird' films of the 60's, devised by Gerry and Sylvia Anderson. The series followed the adventures of International Rescue, an organisation created to help those in grave danger using technically advanced equipment and machinery. Gerry Anderson had been stationed at RAF Manston from 1947 to 1949 for his national service and had witnessed both those events.

Margate and Ramsgate were both popular seaside resorts in the 40's and were just bus rides away. We often enjoyed visits to the beach at Margate and learnt to swim in the sea water pool.

Granny and Granddad frequently came to see us with their little dog, Dinkie. She was a lovely little dog, possibly a cairn terrier, with a shaggy honey coloured coat. While we were waiting for the bus, I would sit in Marilyn's push chair and Dinkie would pull me along like a horse and carriage. We seemed to spend a lot of time waiting for buses. On one occasion I had a brand new skipping rope which I managed to tangle so effectively round the railings at the bus stop that, when the bus eventually came, it was impossible to extricate it and I had to leave it behind!

We always enjoyed visits from Auntie Dot (Mum's sister, Dorothy) and my cousin, Gillian. I also have vivid memories of a visit from Auntie Cissie (Mum's sister, Gladys) which disturbed me for many years to come. We were travelling to Ramsgate on the bus and I was sitting next to Auntie Cissy. As we passed the harbour she pointed out a rather grand red brick building with a large arched doorway. I asked her why the door always seemed to be open. Auntie Cissie explained that it was the house of an evil giant. (That was why it had such a big door). She told me that whenever the giant went out he left the door open in the hope that unwary children would wander in. She said that there was a trapdoor in the middle of the floor and if anyone stepped on it they would fall through into the cellar below. When the giant came home he would close the door behind him and see which one of his captives he would fancy for his tea! Her scary story made a profound impression on me and for many years I really believed that this evil giant existed because I had seen the proof – the house he lived in. I wouldn't go anywhere near that building and it took many years before I realised that Auntie Cissie had spun a cruel and lurid yarn. The building was actually the Old Custom House which, at the time, was used as the Town Hall - and so the door would always be open during normal business hours!

Number 1 Pouces Cottages must have been infested by mice as I remember Mum setting traps baited with cheese. That was probably the reason why we got our first cat, Billy, who would be an important part of our family for the duration of this book. We were so excited! We walked down the road to the neighboring farm where, beside the place where they boiled up the pig swill, was a piece of rusty corrugated iron leaning against some bales of straw. The farmer lifted the sheet and there, warm and cosy, was a nest of tiny tabby kittens. We chose Billy, wrapped him in a woolly blanket and took him home. Although he was a feral kitten and did always have a bit of a wild streak, he grew up to be a lovely family pet.

One of the most exciting events of 1949 was the arrival of the replica Viking ship 'Hugin' at Viking Bay, Broadstairs. It was 24 metres long and sailed with 53 crewmen from Denmark to Thanet to celebrate the 1500th anniversary of the invasion of Britain, the traditional landing of Hengist and Horsa and the betrothal of Hengist's daughter, Rowena, to King Vortigen of Kent. It is now on permanent display on the cliff top at Pegwell Bay, Ramsgate.

Many other events took place at around the same time. Marilyn and I took part in a large fancy dress parade held in Ellington Park at Ramsgate. I went as a doll in a box. I was dressed in a pretty red dress and bonnet, trimmed with white broderie anglais and wearing a large cardboard box – probably the box that once contained Marilyn's pedal car. Marilyn was a fairy and she won the prize for the under 5's section.

As the summer of 1949 drew to a close, the family received some unexpected news. A large council housing estate was being constructed in the outskirts of London. It would be in the area of St. Paul's Cray, between Chislehurst and Orpington - and we were to be allotted one of the 3,000 new houses to be built there.

This was welcome and exciting news. Mum was expecting another baby in March and we all had dreaded the prospect of spending another winter in the cold and draughty cottage. Now we could look forward to starting a new life in a brand new modern house. There would be local shops and schools and it would be much nearer to Dad's work in London. It was time to say goodbye to the smell of rotten cabbages, the possibility of planes crashing into the house, Dad's long cycle ride to Margate station and lengthy train journey to work and, most importantly, the death defying walk across the airfield to cross the runway in order to get to the nearest shop!

CHAPTER 4
1950 - 1954

It was a cold day in January 1950 when we closed the door for the last time on the cold and draughty house at Manston and set off for our new home. Dad had already left with the furniture in the removals van. Mum, Marilyn and I were going to travel by train. I can't recall much about the journey but I do remember standing outside the station at St. Mary Cray where, apparently, Dad was supposed to meet us. The wind was bitter and, after waiting a while, we decided to make our own way to the new house. Mum, dressed in her deep red gabardine coat, was seven months pregnant, Marilyn was only three and I was five. We each carried bags filled with our most precious possessions. Leeson's Hill, which was nothing more than a country lane at the time, was a steep uphill climb and the journey of over 2 miles seemed endless. However we spotted unusual things on the way such as a badger sett in the bank by the side of the road. Eventually Leeson's Hill emerged into Chislehurst woods and we turned right into St. Paul's Wood Hill. After passing some fields on the left and Hoblingwell Wood on the right we came to the brow of the hill where a vast panorama opened up before us. We could see for miles. On the horizon we could see factory chimneys from the distant Medway towns and spread before us was the vast expanse of the newly built St Paul's Cray housing estate. We turned left into Brenchley Road. It was a short road on the very edge of the estate, sloping steeply downhill with only twelve semi-detached houses on each side.

Number 23, our new home, was the end house on the left hand side. We were cold and exhausted but so excited to get inside and explore. It all felt so clean and airy with the smell of new plaster and fresh paint. Dad, who must have met us on the road, had lit the fire, but it took a while for the house to warm through.

I rushed upstairs to see our new bedroom and sat on the low, wide windowsill which, in itself, was an exciting new experience! Looking down through the metal framed Crittall windows I could see our garden. It was just a strangely shaped triangular plot of bare earth, divided from our neighbours by simple chestnut fencing. The house was built of red brick with a red tiled roof. Inside everything, (walls and woodwork), was painted cream.

The front door opened into a small hallway with the stairs straight ahead and the door to the lounge on the left. We had a barometer on the wall which everyone tapped as they passed. As you entered the lounge the window was on the left with an oak extending dining table and chairs beneath. The large matching art deco sideboard was against the adjacent wall. Opposite the window was an open fireplace with a beige tiled surround. On the mantelpiece was a clock flanked by a pair of barley twist candlesticks, under which Dad used to leave the weekly housekeeping money for Mum. In the alcove to the left of the chimney breast was an oak bureau with a matching glazed bookcase above it. We had a beautiful old fashioned piano, with brass candlesticks and intricate inlaid woodwork, on the right hand wall. (Marilyn remembers how our trusted piano tuner, who looked like Mr. Pastry and lived in World's End Lane, was exposed in the local paper as being a con-man and fraudster!) There was a carpet square on the solid floor surrounded by dark coloured polished Marley thermoplastic tiles. A mirror hung on a chain from the wooden picture rail which ran around the walls and the central lampshade was a beige upside-down glass bowl hanging from chains from the ceiling – which was a brilliant fly catcher! We had a standard lamp and two upright parker knoll chairs with wooden arms. We never saw the original upholstery as Mum recovered them, to protect them, as soon as they arrived.

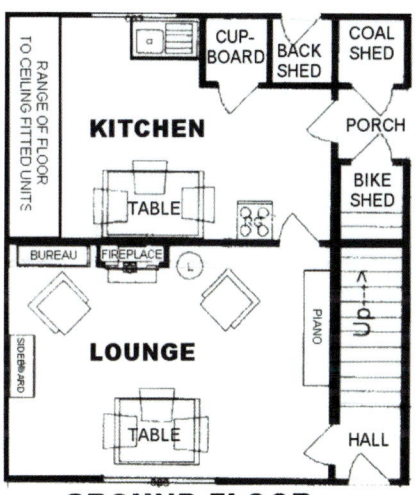

GROUND FLOOR

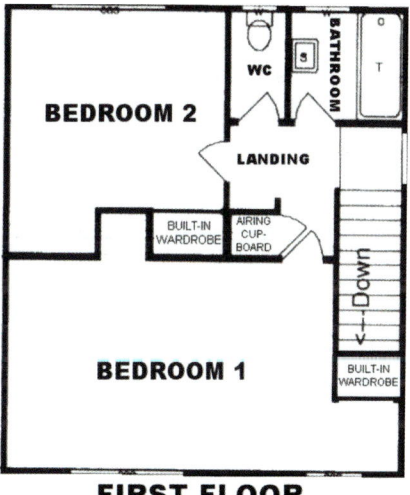

FIRST FLOOR

The kitchen was at the back of the house and was a large bright sunny room. The white butler sink was under the window with a wooden draining board. There was a larder and a range of wooden cupboards. We had a gas stove for cooking and the clothes washing was done with a washboard in a large metal boiler. We had no fridge, so milk bottles were kept in a bowl of cold water draped with a wet cloth in the larder. The kitchen door was on the right and this opened onto a covered porch with steps down to the side of the house. There were doors to storage areas on both sides of the porch. On the left was the coal shed and on the right was a larger storage area under the stairs, where Dad kept his bicycle and which always had a rather pungent odour. This was because Dad would boil up fish heads for Billy, our tabby cat and then leave the aluminium saucepan in that shed to cool down and congeal into a revolting fishy jelly. (He used to buy the fish heads 'up the cut' a London street market near where he worked). It couldn't have been very pleasant for his fellow train passengers when he carried home the dripping parcel wrapped in wet newspaper in the summer heat!

Upstairs there was a small landing with a window overlooking Beddington Road. On the windowsill was a cactus which seemed to shoot its vicious spikes at us as we passed. Turning to the left was the large main bedroom. Later this was split into two with a hardboard partition. Facing you was the airing cupboard and the bathroom and separate toilet were on the right. The second, smaller bedroom was straight ahead. When we first moved in Marilyn and I shared this room although later, when Christine was older, the three of us moved into the larger bedroom. The house, although compact, was well designed with plenty of storage space. It hasn't changed much over the last 70 years and still has our initials carved into the wall beside the front door).

The back of the house faced south so the garden was warm and sunny. Dad soon created a crazy paving patio area and made a rustic seat where Mum could relax and read in the sunshine. We had a swing, which could be covered with a canopy to create a shady area and there was a fish pond. A couple of steps led up to a raised triangular shaped lawn with a shed at the end. We acquired an old rubber dinghy which, filled with water, made a refreshing paddling pool in the hot weather.

Steps went up to the front door and the left side of the front garden was laid to lawn with a border of various beautiful and sweet smelling shrub roses, fed by the copious buckets of manure Dad collected from the  milkman's horse! He loved his roses and there were climbing varieties on the front of the house and growing through the rustic trellis around the garden. A cherry tree was planted on the right side. The entire front and side gardens were bordered by well-trimmed privet hedges.

Soon after moving to St Paul's Cray, Marilyn and I were sent off to Croydon to stay with Granny while Mum was giving birth to Christine. She was born at home on the 21st March 1950. They had no car or telephone so Dad had to rush off on his bike to fetch the midwife. Mum was left alone until the midwife arrived - just in the nick of time.

We were with Granny at the time of the annual boat race, which seemed to be a very important event in Croydon. Everyone wore brooches or badges with either light blue or dark blue feathers – depending on which side they supported. I chose dark blue (which was for Oxford) but on that occasion, 1st April 1950, the race was won by the crew from Cambridge University.

Croydon had been badly bombed in the war and many buildings were destroyed. Bomb sites were everywhere and it didn't seem unusual to have to pick our way across piles of rubble. We travelled around the town by rickety old-fashioned trams and trolley buses. On one occasion I was waiting at the  bus stop with Granny, who was chatting to a fellow passenger. I made a remark about a certain 'lady' in the distance. The person with Granny, who had the demeanour of a school mistress, rebuked me, "You must *never* call anyone a 'lady' unless they have a title. That person is a 'woman'. Never forget that!" She then opened her purse and gave me a silver sixpence. I protested, as Mum always did when someone gave her anything, saying, "I couldn't possibly ..." while expecting her to insist that I keep it. To my surprise and disappointment she took back the coin saying, "If someone has the decency to give you something you should always accept it gratefully". I never did get that sixpence but I did learn two very important lessons that day which I never forgot - female people should be called 'women' unless they really are 'ladies' and any gifts that are offered should be gratefully received!

After Christine was born we returned home and I had to start attending a new school. The nearest primary school was Grays Farm Infants School which was over a mile away. For an unaccompanied 7 year old it was a long uphill walk back up Midfield Way, St Paul's Wood Hill and Beddington Road and it was often dark by the time I finally got home that winter.

When we moved to St Paul's Cray, building work on the estate was still in progress and there were no nearby amenities such as shops, schools or churches for the new residents.

Mum wanted us to have a good religious upbringing so she took us to the nearest church which was St. Nicholas in Chislehurst. This was a beautiful medieval church built of knapped flint which contained the tomb of Thomas Walsingham (1561-1630) who had lived at the nearby Scadbury  Manor. There was no transport so the only way to get there was a long walk through Chislehurst woods. Christine was christened there and we were sent regularly to Sunday school where, each week, a little picture was stuck on a card to prove that we had attended.

We never really felt at ease in that church. The vicar and the congregation were not very welcoming (they probably resented the intrusion of people like us from the council estate into their upper-crust world). One day there was a knock on the door and a young woman was standing on the doorstep. She was Eileen Beardow, a young pioneer sister from Chislehurst Congregation of Jehovah's Witnesses. Mum was very spiritually minded and had a long discussion with Eileen on the doorstep while we were freezing inside. For all her life Mum had sought answers to deep questions such as; what is the meaning of life; what does the future hold and why is there so much suffering in the world? Despite a lifetime of going to church her questions were never answered. Eileen was able to show her that satisfying answers to her questions could be found in God's Word the Bible. Mum was amazed by what she heard and agreed that Eileen could come back and begin to study the Bible with her.

Eileen lived miles away in Mottingham but regularly cycled to St Paul's Cray where quite a number of the new residents wanted to learn more about the Bible. Later she bravely started a study group for some of their children at the home of Bob and Grace Affleck, just down the hill at the bottom of Beddington Road. She attempted to teach us about the Bible using the study aid 'Let God be True'. We were quite an unruly group and she had a hard time trying to get us to concentrate on what was actually quite complicated material. Unlike today, there were no books designed specifically for children.

The meetings were held in a rented hall above the Co-op shop in Chislehurst. Mum wouldn't take me to her first meeting but she came back almost glowing. "The people are so lovely," she said. "They are like a big family. They call each other 'brothers and sisters'!"

The next meeting was on a Thursday evening and this time Mum let me go with her. I don't actually remember much about it but Marilyn, who wasn't allowed to go, remembers staying awake, waiting for me to return so she could find out what happened. I was so excited by what I had learnt. "I know something that you don't know. I bet you didn't know that God has a name?" Marilyn thought for a while before answering. "Yes I do. I think his name is Harold!" I was puzzled. "Why do you think that?" I asked. "Because at school we say, 'Our Father, which art in heaven, Harold be thy name!'" I explained that at the meeting we had learnt that the Bible tells us that God's name is 'Jehovah' and, when we say the Lord's Prayer we are actually praying for God's name, Jehovah, to be hallowed which means sanctified. I was able to prove it to her by showing her Psalm 83:18.

Although she was very busy with three young children, Mum enjoyed her Bible study and was convinced that, after a lifetime of searching, she had finally found the truth. Unfortunately Dad wasn't too keen and did his best to discourage her. He had heard some very weird things about Jehovah's Witnesses and didn't want her to get involved with them. Despite his strong opposition, she was determined to persevere and eventually he was able to see for himself that the things he had been told were completely untrue and that, because she was now applying Bible principles in her life, Mum had become a much better and happier person. Gradually he became more tolerant, although it would be many years later before he actually decided to study for himself.

My best friend was Gloria Webb, who lived in a cul-de-sac at the top of Beddington Road. I used to go round to her house after school and watch television. Her family was one of the first in our area to own a set in those days. We enjoyed watching Children's Hour, especially programmes such as 'Muffin the Mule' with Annette Mills, and Andy Pandy. One of my most treasured toys was a Muffin the mule string puppet which Granny had given me. We all used to play safely in the street as there were very few cars.

My favourite book was 'Black Beauty'. I loved everything to do with horses and ponies. I yearned to have a pony of my own but with our circumstances I knew it could never really happen. However, Mum did save up some of her hard earned housekeeping money and let me have a few lessons at Chislehurst riding school. Even though I didn't have the proper attire I felt on top of the world! I rode Twinkle and Merrylegs, both little grey ponies with big personalities. We would trek along the bridle paths through the beautiful Petts Woods, past the Willett memorial. This was a sundial erected to commemorate William Willett – the man who first came up with the idea of British Summer Time. William Willett was a prominent Edwardian builder who lived in Chislehurst. A keen supporter of outdoor activities, he noticed that during the summer, people were still sleeping when the sun had risen. Willett began to think about changing the nation's clocks and published his idea in a pamphlet called 'A waste of daylight'. Although William died before his ideas were adopted, it was his pamphlet that paved the way for British Summer Time which was finally adopted in 1916.

Unfortunately we couldn't afford to continue my riding lessons but I was still horse mad and read every book about them I could find. Each year Granny gave me the Pony Club Annual and, in theory, I probably knew everything there was to know about horses and ponies. To have my own horse was always a dream but one which sadly never ever happened.

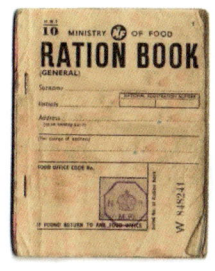

As more people moved onto the estate, additional amenities were being provided. A small parade of six shops was built in Leith Hill which wasn't too far to walk and, as long as we had enough stamps in our ration books, would provide the basic necessities. A new primary school was being built at the top of St Paul's Wood Hill. At first there were just a few temporary wooden huts but later the proper school was finished and could be accessed from the top of Beddington Road, which was very convenient for us.

My first class at St Paul's Wood Hill School with our teacher, Mr. Simpson.

1951

One of the most exciting and memorable events of 1951 was the Festival of Britain. This was a national exhibition and fair in London that was visited by millions in the summer of 1951. Labour cabinet member Herbert Morrison was the prime mover; in 1947 he started with the original plan to celebrate the centennial of the Great Exhibition of 1851. However it was not to be another World Fair, for international themes were absent. Instead the 1951 festival focused entirely on Britain and its achievements; it was funded chiefly by the government, with a budget of £12 million. The Labour government was losing support and so the implicit goal of the festival was to give the people a feeling of successful recovery from the war's devastation, as well as promoting British science, technology, industrial design, architecture and the arts.

The main site featured the 'Dome of Discovery', the largest dome in the world at the time, standing 93 feet tall with a diameter of 365 feet. This held exhibitions on the theme of discovery such as the New World, the Polar Regions, the Sea, the Sky and Outer Space. It also included a 12-ton steam engine on show. However the exhibit that I remember most and which really terrified me was the huge skeleton of some prehistoric beast. Adjacent to the Dome was the Skylon, a breathtaking, iconic and futuristic-looking structure. The Skylon was an unusual, vertical cigar shaped tower supported by cables that gave the impression that it was floating above the ground. Some say this structure mirrored the British economy of the time having no clear means of support.

Another feature was the Telekinema, a 400-seat state-of-the-art cinema operated by the British Film Institute. This had the necessary technology to screen both films (including 3D films) and large screen television. Other buildings at the Festival site on the South Bank of the Thames included the Royal Festival Hall, a 2,900 seat concert hall that hosted concerts conducted by the likes of Sir Malcolm Sargent and Sir Adrian Boult; a new wing of the Science Museum and the Exhibition of Live Architecture at Poplar.

For me, at the age of 8, the most enjoyable part of the Festival of Britain was the Pleasure Garden in Battersea Park. This contained a large and amazing funfair with all sorts of rides and open-air amusements. There was a gigantic big-dipper, an enormous water chute which guaranteed a good soaking and then there was the Rotor. This was a large, upright barrel which rotated at 33 revolutions per minute. The rotation of the barrel created a centrifugal effect. Once the barrel had attained full speed, the floor was retracted, leaving the riders stuck high up on the wall of the drum. At the end of the ride, the drum slowed down and gravity took over as the riders slid slowly down the wall. I thought it was magic that it was possible to be suspended about 20 feet from the ground!

My favourite ride was the Far Tottering and Oyster Creek Branch Railway. This was a narrow gauge railway created by Rowland Emett, based on his cartoons from Punch magazine in the 30's. There were three locomotives, Nellie, Neptune and Wild Goose and two stations, each as whimsical as the locomotives. I loved that fantastical little railway and for the rest of that summer we endeavoured to emulate Emett's vision in our own back garden. We gathered together all the chairs we could muster and with various umbrellas, assorted household gadgets and any other interesting objects that we found; we created our very own whimsical railway.

In the picture below, my friend June Beadle was driving 'Nellie' with a kettle providing the steam. Gloria Webb, complete with handbag, was sitting behind her. Marilyn was the driver of 'Neptune' and I was her passenger.

1952 began with some sad news. On the 6th February we were in the middle of a history lesson with Mr. Simpson (still in the huts at the top of St Paul's Wood Hill) when Mr. Webb, the headmaster, came in and interrupted the class with a rather sombre expression on his face. "I have some very grave news," he announced. "His majesty King George VI died peacefully in his sleep at Sandringham House in the early hours of this morning". It came as a shock to everyone. The King was only 56 but had been suffering from a worsening lung condition. His daughter, the young Princess Elizabeth, was now our new queen.

 In the summer of 1952 we spent a lot of time with Granny and Grandad and we also went on holiday to Paignton. The highlight was a visit to Kent's Cavern in Torquay but that had unfortunate consequences. We think Mum scratched her leg in the caves; the tiny scratch became infected and she became seriously ill with cellulitis.

She had a high temperature and her leg was very inflamed. It took a long while for it to heal and caused permanent damage that affected her for the rest of her life.

Because Dad was only on a very low income, Mum made all our clothes and we were particularly proud of our Scottish kilts made of genuine woollen tartan.

1952

She also made the costumes for a fancy dress competition at a fete held in a field at the bottom of Midfield way. I was dressed as a gypsy, Marilyn was Little Miss Muffet, complete with spider, and Christine went as a fairy.

Fancy Dress at Midfield Fete
1952

Mum was baptised in 1952 at the district convention held at Mitcham stadium, near London.

Mum's Baptism at Mitcham Stadium
1952

By now Marilyn and I were attending the meetings with her, which were still being held in the hall above the Co-op shop in Chislehurst. We went on a Thursday evening to the Ministry School and Service meeting and on Sunday afternoon to the public talk and Watchtower study. Sometimes the public talks were held in the open air beside Chislehurst pond. On a Tuesday evening there was a study group at the home of Bob and Grace Affleck in Beddington Road, just down the road from us. As mentioned earlier, Eileen Beardow arranged for a children's Bible study, also held at the Affleck's house. There were quite a few of us – Lillian and Jeanette Affleck; Ruth, Pam, Barney and Paul Adams as well as Marilyn and me. We weren't the easiest bunch and she must have had quite a job to keep us in order!

The big event of 1953 was the coronation of Queen Elizabeth II on the 2nd June in Westminster Abbey. Her Majesty was the thirty-ninth Sovereign to be crowned at Westminster Abbey. For some reason we decided that it would be a good day to have a trip to the seaside at Margate. (Probably because we thought it would be quiet as everybody would be at home watching the coronation on their newly purchased television sets). Unfortunately it was a horrible day – the weather was miserable; wet and really cold. The only way we could keep warm was to stand as close as possible to a hog roast that was being cooked on a spit over an open fire in Dreamland!

Granny and Granddad came to visit us every three weeks. They came on the Green Line coach and we would often walk through the woods to

meet them at the bus stop near Chislehurst war memorial. They were very generous and always bought Mum a bunch of flowers from their garden and presents and comics for us. At first we had the Beano, Dandy and Topper and then, as we got older, graduated to The Girl and School Friend. One of my favourite presents was a large Teddy Bear which I still treasure today, although after nearly 70 years he is now a little threadbare!

Granny worked as a cleaner at Grants, a large department store in Croydon and Granddad was a dustman. They saved up throughout the year for their annual fortnight's holiday - which they generously shared with Marilyn and me. Each summer we would go and stay with them; usually I had the first week and Marilyn the second. We did something exciting everyday of that holiday. When it was over it must have been quite restful for them to go back to work! They took us to places such as Chessington Zoo and Battersea Park on the train and to the seaside by coach.

The coaches were called 'charabancs' and there was always a stop on the journey at the 'half-way house' where the men would enjoy a pint of frothy beer and the women would gossip over a 'nice cup of tea'! We went for day trips to most of the seaside towns on the south coast; Ramsgate, Margate, Hastings, Eastbourne, Littlehampton, Brighton and probably many more. When we arrived we usually went straight to the amusement park where Grandad would take us on scary rides. There were terrifying big dippers at the Kursaal in

Southend and at Dreamland in Margate as well as the huge one at Battersea park. I learned later that Grandad had a heart condition – but that didn't seem to deter him! We would eat jellied eels, cockles and mussels and I had to be taught how to extricate whelks from their shells using a pin. Most of the seaside towns had a pier, lined with all sorts of amusements and 'what the butler saw' type machines. I would be dragged away from the booths selling colourful saucy postcards and we always went home loaded with prizes from the various fairground stalls. I recall once winning a beautiful doll dressed as a bride and, on another occasion, a rather garish bone china tea set. Late one night we were travelling back from Brighton when Granny told me that we were on the newly built duel-carriageway. I thought she had said 'jewel carriageway' as, stretched ahead of us in the darkness, the cat's eyes bordering the road resembled a string of glittering diamonds. For many years after that I insisted that any road with cat's eyes was called a 'jewel carriageway' and nobody could persuade me otherwise!

In 1953 I started my first business venture. The golden hamster - an attractive small, furry rodent from Syria - had recently been introduced into this country and was about to become a popular pet. Dad made a wooden cage (a green painted love-nest with a little nameplate, 'Rose Cottage') for Goldie and her husband and it seemed a wonderful opportunity to get on the hamster bandwagon! Goldie duly produced seven babies and everything was going well.

My cousin, Gillian was to be my first customer and, as soon as the baby was old enough, we carefully packed him into a box and took him on the long journey to Cheam. (It wasn't far as the crow flies but it did involve catching four different buses). Auntie Dot and Uncle Alf had provided a nice little cage and Gillian was thrilled at the prospect of having a new pet. With great anticipation we opened the box and, to our horror, the terrified little creature jumped out and landed on the floor. Unfortunately I stepped backwards - with disastrous consequences - and from then on my hamster breeding programme lost its initial appeal.

By 1953 the new St Paul's Wood Hill junior school had been completed and could be accessed from steps at the top of Beddington Road. The original huts were now being used as the infant's school. I now had a wonderful teacher, Mr. Hills. Mr. Simpson (my first teacher in that school) was renowned for his use of 'the slipper' as a punishment for the slightest misdemeanor. Naughty pupils had to bend over and were wacked by his white plimsole shoe! He was also prone to throw the blackboard rubber at anyone who wasn't paying attention. Even Mr. Webb, the headmaster was not averse to using the cane as punishment. However, Mr. Hills did not need to resort to either and I did quite well in his class, particularly in art and academic subjects.

One thing I was not very good at was knitting and the thought of the dreadful yellow scarf saga still haunts me today. Several years earlier, when I first went to the junior school, I was in Miss Bratbury's class and she taught us how to knit. We were given some wool and were supposed to knit  a scarf. Unlike the other (sensible) children who used a simple pattern, I wanted to be different and decided to use moss stitch to give a more textured effect. That was a fundamental mistake as it was a far more complicated stitch and took a lot of concentration. It requires you to complete one row of "knit one, purl one", followed by the next of "purl one, knit one", and so on. Whereas most people finished their scarves in no time, mine was a nightmare and I was still struggling with it many years later. In fact, Marilyn reminded me that when I was about to leave the school it still wasn't finished and my teacher had to complete it for me. I never wanted to see a pair of knitting needles again!

Apart from knitting and gym I was often top of my group in Mr. Hill's class and passed with flying colors when we took the exam to decide on our next school

The nearest established grammar school was Chislehurst and Sidcup and I was sent for an interview at that school. I remember being asked what career I hoped to pursue and told them I would like to become a teacher or a nurse. Thinking back, I probably would have been hopeless at either! As it happened, there was talk of a new grammar school being opened in Orpington as a response to the needs generated by the rapid growth of the surrounding area over the previous years. The idea went ahead although, as yet, there was no school building.

I was privileged to win a place in the first single form entry which was to be housed temporarily in Midfield Secondary School for girls. We had our own school uniform which, in winter, was a bottle green gymslip, cream blouse and green cardigan with a green gabardine coat and a beret with the school badge. In summer we had a green and white check dress with a straw hat and bottle green blazer.  The school badge was an acorn with two oak leaves symbolizing how big things grow from little beginnings. The school motto was 'Fortitudine Crescamus' which means 'May We Grow in Strength'. The school is now called Newstead Woods but the badge is still the same.

I left the junior school at the end of the summer term and on the 24th July 1954, since I was about to start the senior school, I was considered old enough to be baptised at the district assembly in Luton.

Our form mistress at the new school was a very formidable woman – Miss Irene Payne. She was very strict and I, at least, was very frightened of her. She taught mathematics, which was my worse subject, but she was determined that I would successfully pass the final exams. Despite her stern and severe demeanor I know that she really had our best interests at heart and was an excellent teacher - although she certainly didn't suffer fools gladly or wouldn't tolerate any bad behavior – and nobody would even dare to try!

We were at Midfield until 1957 when our own school building in Orpington was finally completed and, apart from Miss Payne, we were taught by their teachers. Mrs. Shaw was the headmistress and she taught us Latin, which at that time was my favourite subject. Another notable teacher was Miss Lee, a real character, who taught history and ballroom dancing. I did especially well during those years and won two prizes; a book about wild flowers in the first year, which was a prize for improvement, and in the second year, after coming top in all the exams, I won a wonderful encyclopedia – the prize for good work.

CHAPTER 5
1955 – 1959

By 1955 Christine had started infant's school, Marilyn was in the juniors and I was at Orpington Grammar School for Girls.

I was awarded a very useful book called 'Wild flowers of the Wayside and Woodland. (The underlining on the prize certificate was done by Christine, who also coloured in most of the black and white drawings in the book!

Holland 1955

In the summer of 1955 there was a series of international assemblies and we were very privileged that we could attend the one at The Hague in Holland. This was the first time we had been abroad and it was all very exciting.

Here are a few photos of our garden and a visit to Cheam to visit Nanny.

Nanny, my Mum's mother, shared a house at 73 Priory Crescent, Cheam, Surrey with Auntie Dot, Uncle Alf and my cousin Gillian. They had a little black and white terrier type dog. We used to visit them about once every month. It was a convoluted journey; we had to take the 61 bus to Chislehurst where we caught the green line to Croydon. We then caught another bus to Cheam village and a further one to their nearest bus stop, where we then walked to their house. Gillian was an excellent swimmer and I would often accompany her to the nearby swimming baths, where I learnt to swim. They had a television set and we all would all enjoy watching the Saturday afternoon wrestling before starting the long journey back home.

Nanny died in June 1956 at the age of 81. I remember that there were some beautiful horse chestnut trees in full bloom near the hospital that looked as though they had been decorated with candles! Nanny, Sarah Mundon, was born in the reign of Queen Victoria and had a hard life. She was suddenly widowed in her 40's and had to bring up her four daughters alone. She lived through two world wars and had six grandchildren – all girls. (Auntie Cissy had Pamela, Auntie Dot had Gillian, Auntie Eddie had Jacqueline and Mum had us three).

I didn't enjoy getting wet and muddy playing hockey in the winter time at school. I much preferred tennis and that summer Dad fixed up a contraption in the side garden to enable me to practice on my own. He strung a rope between 2 poles and attached the ball on a length of elastic. Occasionally the elastic broke and the ball shot off down the hill but surprisingly it usually worked well and helped me develop my strokes.

Jersey 1956

Jersey, the largest of the Channel Islands, had special memories for Mum and Dad as it was the place where they first met. Dad was on a very low wage but because he worked for British railways he was entitled to several free tickets for our family to travel abroad by train and ferry. (This was the only way we could have afforded to go to Holland the previous year).

The journey on the boat train to Southampton was interesting as we were able to watch a partial eclipse of the moon; however the sea crossing was not so good. It was quite a long trip of about seven hours and the sea was rough. We were glad to get ashore and the isle of Jersey certainly lived up to expectations. Although part of Great Britain it felt very different. The sea was a deep blue and there were flowers everywhere. It seemed strange that only a few years previously the island had been occupied by the Nazi Germans during the war. Nearly all the gun emplacements and concrete bunkers were still in existence. One of the most fascinating places we visited was the German underground hospital. This was an amazing feat of engineering, achieved by a massive slave force that was marched from every corner of conquered Europe. Those tunnels were hewn in human misery and suffering and I can still remember the chill we felt as we entered the echoing entrance and were reminded of the many who did not survive.

We stayed in a guest house in St Helier and travelled around the island by bus, exploring the many picturesque bays and coves. Bouley Bay was one beautiful place that had special memories for Mum and Dad.

Later that year my school arranged for our form to spend a week at Juniper Hall, an 18th-century country house leased from the National Trust and used for science and geographical studies. It was the first time I had been away from home without my family. I felt quite nervous at the prospect but actually we had a wonderful time. Back then I used to enjoy reading books about the exciting adventures of schoolgirls in boarding schools (I had the complete series of Chalet School books by Elinor Brent-Dyer) - and this was a similar experience! We slept in dormitories and enjoyed midnight feasts, just like the girls in my books. Miss Payne, our formidable form mistress got on very well with Mr.

Hutchings who was the Warden of the Field Study Centre and she seemed a much nicer person away from the normal school environment.

Mr. Hutchings was a fantastic teacher and a marvelous artist. Whenever we were out on field trips he would do wonderful pencil sketches of the landscape. He drew one for me of the tower on top of Leith Hill. I learned later that he was a well- known illustrator of books, such as these.

In November the following year we had rather a memorable short break in Belgium. The weather was atrocious and I remember paddling through puddles in the torrential rain looking for the accommodation we had booked. When we left home, nobody had noticed that Christine was wearing her flimsy sandals! We finally found our hotel and huddled around a huge Belgium stove drinking hot chocolate in an attempt to get warm and dry out. The weather was better the following day and we enjoyed exploring the picturesque old town of Bruges with its many canals and beautiful buildings.

We had enjoyed our previous holiday in Jersey so much that we went back in 1958. We became very friendly with a sister called Doris Day who we met at the Kingdom Hall. She had two daughters, Susan and Marilyn, who were about the same ages as me and Marilyn. Towards the end of our holiday Marilyn met up with her friend Marilyn and they decided to sit on the beach preparing for the next congregational meeting. We were also by the sea that day and noticed that something, some sort of emergency, was happening further along the beach. We didn't think much more about it until that evening when we were having tea in the conservatory of the guesthouse. There was a knock on the door and it was the police. Marilyn had suffered a very serious accident and she was in intensive care in the hospital. Apparently she and her friend had been sitting on the beach when some youths were messing about and decided to throw rocks from the cliffs above. One of the rocks struck her on the head, fracturing her skull and causing massive blood loss. It seemed unlikely that she would survive. The nursing staff was wonderful and Marilyn did make a miraculous recovery against all the odds. They actually admitted that the reason she healed so quickly was probably because she had refused a blood transfusion with all its inherent risks.

Marilyn remained in hospital for a number of weeks before being flown home by air ambulance. Mum and Chris had stayed on in Jersey with Doris Day but Dad and I needed to get back to work and school.

Jersey 1958

As mentioned earlier my school, Orpington Grammar School for girls, opened in 1954 and I was part of the original intake that were in temporary accommodation at Midfield secondary School for Girls. Building work for our new school in Newstead Road Orpington began in 1955 and was completed in 1957. The picture below is of the new school when it was first built although now it has been vastly extended.

The school moved into those premises on 23rd September 1957. The first head teacher was Miss H.M. Pipe, who served from 1957 until December 1978. The official opening was held on 18th July 1958 by Mrs. Mary Stocks, former Principal of Westfield College, University of London. Apart from Miss Payne, we had a whole new range of teachers; some were excellent but others had come straight from teaching college and were less experienced. Previously I had been very good at Latin and history but it wasn't the same with the new teachers and I reluctantly dropped those subjects. For my forthcoming GCE exams I concentrated on Mathematics, English, French, Biology, Geography and Art.

My favourite subjects were Biology and Art. I always found Mathematics very difficult but Miss Payne was determined that I would pass my final exam – and she succeeded!

Up until now we had been part of Chislehurst congregation but the number of Witness families living on our estate had increased and a new St. Paul's Cray congregation was formed. We used to rent the Moose Hall at the bottom of The Landway, St. Mary Cray, Among the members of the congregation were the Adams family, the Afflecks, the Vineys, the O'Neills, the Emerys, the Hastings, the Bookers and Mum's special friend, a lovely elderly sister called Maud Dale. I will always remember the time when sisters were first allowed to give talks in the Ministry School and I was assigned the very first one. I used to practice for hours with my notes on the music stand of our old piano! Marilyn's first talk was also quite memorable. It was about Hezekiah and Sennacherib and the angelic destruction of 185,000 of the invading Assyrian army. Describing what occurred, she stated, quite seriously, "When they woke up in the morning they found they were all dead!" Everyone laughed and she got the giggles!

The British branch office had recently been completed at Mill Hill, in north London and we arranged a congregation tour to experience the love and skill of the Bethel Family as well as the wonderful facilities of the new factory and home.

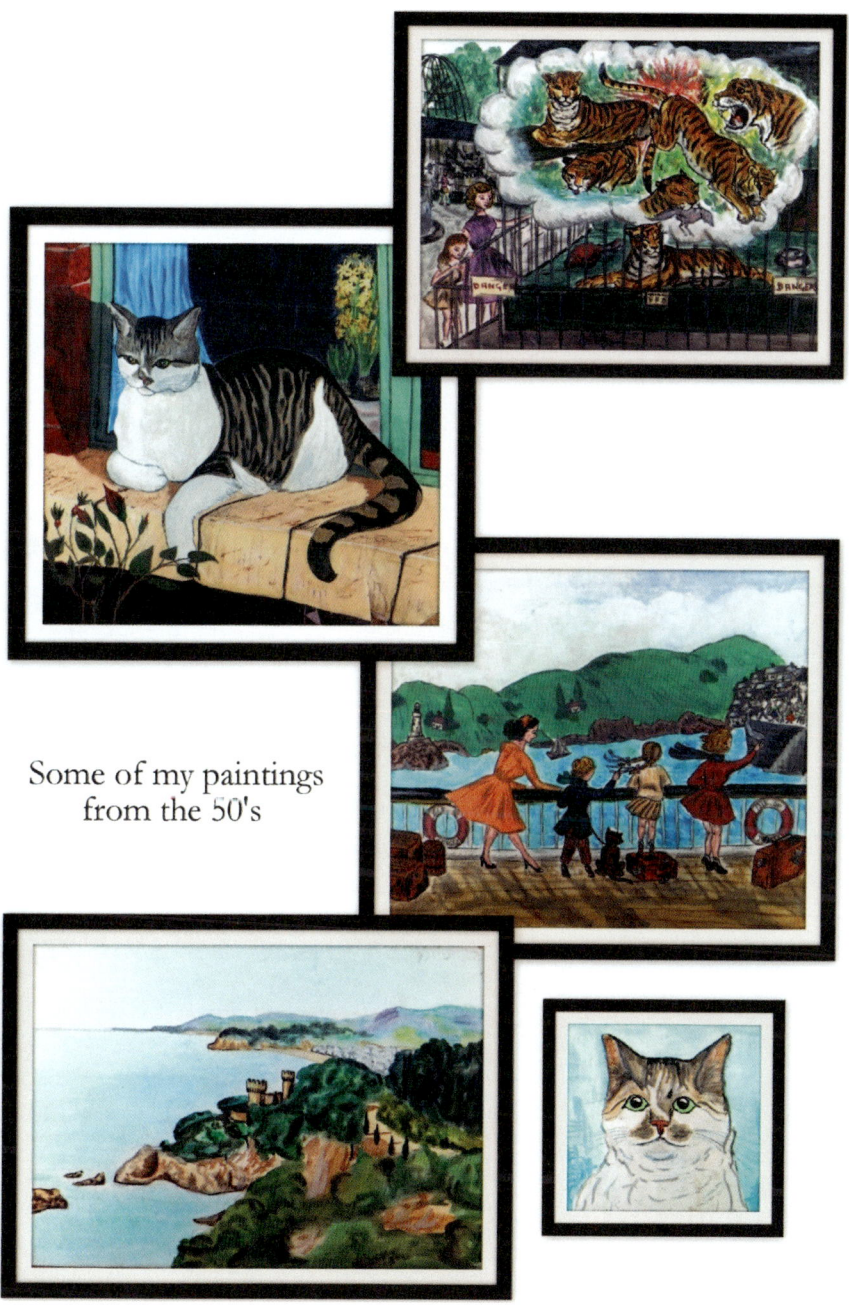

Some of my paintings from the 50's

Art was one my favourite subjects at school and Miss Reeves, our art teacher, entered some of my pen and ink botanical sketches into a national competition. Amazingly this drawing of purple crocuses won an award.

In the summer of 1959 I took my final CCE exams. Most of my classmates went on to the 6th form but due to my family's financial circumstances it was necessary for me to get a job. My Dad was still working for British Railways but, by this time, he had made quite a name for himself developing a special ultrasonic device for detecting cracked rails. He worked in the Permanent Way Section of The Chief Engineer's Department. Knowing that I enjoyed drawing, he arranged for me to have an interview for the position of a tracer and I was offered a job in the drawing office of the Modernisation Department.

Before starting my new job, we had a family holiday to Rimini, on the Adriatic coast of Italy.

It was all very exciting. As a railway employee, Dad was able to get us all free international train tickets. We travelled on 'The Golden Arrow', the boat train between Victoria and Dover and then took the ferry to Calais where we joined the 'Fleche d'Or' to the Gare du Nord in Paris. We then had to travel across Paris to the Gare de Lyon where we caught the Orient Express. Although now this train is synonymous with luxurious and expensive travel, back then in the 50's, it was a normal international sleeper train service which ran between Paris and Istanbul. It left Paris every evening and travelled through the night. The journey took us across France and Switzerland and through the Simplon tunnel, which at over 12 miles was the longest tunnel in the world at that time. As dawn broke there was a distinct chill in the air. I remember shivering as I pulled back the curtains to discover we were travelling through the Alps. I had never seen a mountain before and was completely awestruck by the size of these immense snowcapped mountains. By midmorning the train arrived had at Milan in Northern Italy. While we waited for our connection to Rimini we sat in a little café outside the station and I had my first alcoholic drink. It was a Martini with ice and a slice of lemon – and I can still remember the distinctive taste!

I did this sketch of the small hotel called the Ali d'Oro where we stayed in Rimini. While there we became so friendly with Renato and Marucca who worked there that, when we got home, we named our new pet rabbits after them! We had a lovely holiday in Rimini. We spent most of the time on the beach looking forward to the arrival of the 'Gelati Man' with his amazing Tutti Frutti ice cream!

The highlight of the holiday was a trip to San Marino which is the world's oldest republic and Europe's third smallest state. It lies 657 m above sea level with spectacular views of the surrounding countryside and Adriatic coast, and is situated only 10km from Rimini.

San Marino 1959

Rimini
1959

We had a lovely holiday in Rimini but it was over all too quickly and soon after our return I had to start work at my new job with British Railways.

Getting to London for an 8.30am start proved to be quite a challenge! I had to leave home soon after 6am to walk to the bus stop to catch the 61 bus to Chislehurst war memorial and then take the 227 to Chislehurst station where I then caught the train to Waterloo. Dad used to cycle to the station in all weathers and he would always be there before me. We both worked at South Side Offices which were a cluster of temporary buildings just down the line from Waterloo Station. Dad worked in the Permanent Way section and I was in an adjacent building in the Modernisation section, both part of the Chief Civil Engineer's Department. Dad started off as a lowly platelayer but by the time I joined he had made quite a name for himself developing a machine that had the potential to save thousands of lives. It was an ultrasonic rail testing device that could detect the smallest crack or flaw inside the rail. He gave lectures and wrote technical papers about this innovative and very specialised invention.

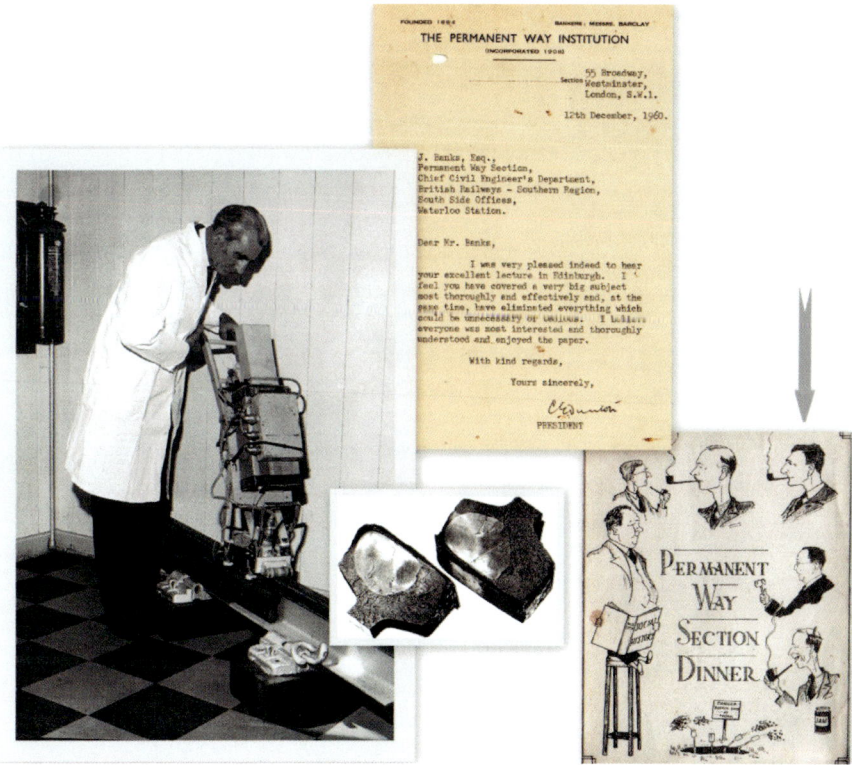

I worked as a tracer in the drawing office with Carole and Wendy, who were both 19 and very grown-up, and the head tracer, Connie Warburton. The draughtsmen would draw the plans and our job would be to accurately trace them with Indian ink on to specially prepared blue linen. It was skilled and demanding work; mistakes couldn't be made as it was impossible to erase the ink. Drawings and text had to be perfect in every way. The tracings would then be printed onto cartridge paper and we would colour them in with watercolour washes. Everything was colour coded and all the proposed new projects would be coloured pink. We worked accompanied by the radio which would be playing the hit song of the year – 'Only Sixteen' by Craig Douglas which, of course, everyone dedicated to me!

When I started work we had a long hot Indian summer and at lunchtime we would take our chairs outside and eat our sandwiches beside the tracks, waving to the drivers of the huge steam locomotives as they roared past, picking up speed as they pulled out of Waterloo station. Sometimes we would catch the tube to shop in Oxford Street or meander through 'The Cut' which was a nearby street market filled with Cockney stallholders.

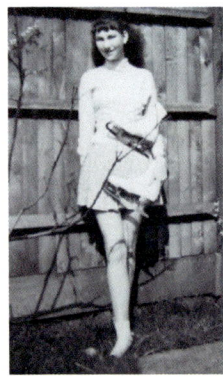

The change from school to work was a bit of a shock to the system. At first I found the long days and all the travelling to London very tiring until I became accustomed to it. My wages were just over £4 per week, but I did have free rail travel to work and a number of other free tickets, including international rail travel, each year. The disadvantage, although it seemed normal at the time, was that almost everyone smoked constantly in the office and on the packed commuter trains so it was impossible not to suffer the effects of the toxic smoke filled atmosphere.

Once a week, after work, I met up with Ann Freeman, one of my friends from school, and we went skating at Streatham Ice Rink.

I was anxious to know my exam results and finally, in November 1959, I received a letter from the school confirming that I had passed all six subjects. I was delighted but I knew Miss Payne must have been very satisfied that she had achieved the impossible!

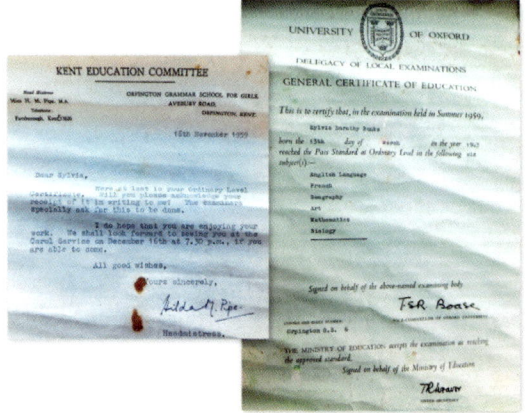

CHAPTER 6
1960 – 1965

The 1960's were probably the most interesting and exciting years of my life as I accomplished so many things in such a short time; I worked in London for British Railways, pioneered, had several boyfriends, became self-employed, travelled to exciting places, got married, had children and finally moved from Kent to the Cotswolds.

Up to about 1960 we had been living rather frugally as Dad was on quite a low wage. However I think, because of his life-saving project, he must have had a pay rise. For the first time we were able to afford things that previously we could only dream about. We replaced our ancient wireless set with a polished wooden radiogram complete with just one single 78 record – 'Volare', sung by Dean Martin and very popular at time. Soon after that we bought a television set and watched the very first episode of Doctor Who. We then had a telephone installed and, when I finally passed my driving test, we bought our first car – but more about that later!

My journey to work in 1960 was very different to travelling today. I waited on the platform at Chislehurst station for the train from Sevenoaks to Charing Cross. It was an electric train painted in Southern Region's dark green livery. There was no corridor and each coach comprised of individual compartments with a door on either side and bench seats facing each other with a luggage rack above. The trains were very crowded and I would be lucky to get a seat. Sometimes there were so many people standing that it was difficult to slam the doors. Most of the men who worked in the city wore bowler hats and carried rolled umbrellas. It was quite a sight to see the army of smartly dressed, bowler hatted gents crossing Waterloo Bridge on their way to work

I loved the very feminine fashion styles of that era. The dresses were mid-calf length with very full skirts, tight fitting bodices and nipped in waists worn with high heeled shoes and layers and layers of stiff net petticoats. I designed my own dresses, bought the material and Mum made them up. Gingham trimmed with broderie anglais was very popular at the time. For work we wore rather figure hugging sweaters and slim pencil skirts.

In the summer of 1960 we had our first family holiday to Spain. We travelled on the sleeper train to Port Bou and then took a local train onwards to the Costa Brava.

We stayed at the Hotel El Dragon in Lloret de Mar which, at that time, was a quaint and lovely little town but apparently is now a major resort. Beehive hairstyles were fashionable back then and the lady who owned the hotel had her bright auburn hair arranged in the biggest beehive I had ever seen. We had a lovely time in Spain, swimming in the lovely warm Mediterranean Sea in the day time and enjoying the music and dancing in the town square in the evening – but it was over all too soon and I had to go back to work.

I enjoyed working in the Modernisation Section. It was a large office, filled with hunky draughtsmen, and our small tracing section was at one end. We each had our own drawing board and our work mostly consisted of drawing the planned new projects or updating older ones. One of the most interesting proposals for the future, and one that seemed impossible at the time, was the construction of a Channel Tunnel. We had the opportunity to go to see a model of the projected design – but no one believed it was feasible or could ever be achieved. In fact it was thirty years later before anyone took it seriously! One of my favourite jobs was tracing the original old plans (which were in poor condition and beginning to crumble) of some of the more interesting London station buildings. I loved drawing all the intricate architectural details and embellishments of these elaborate Victorian designs.

There was a young man working as a trainee draughtsman in my office whose name was Rodney Tillstone-LaTrobe. He was nineteen and lived in Reigate where his parents owned a toyshop. He had recently graduated from Whitgift College, a prestigious public school near Croydon and appeared to be very spiritually minded. He had begun to study the Bible with Wally Whisker, a brother originally from my congregation but who had moved to Redhill, and we would often spend our lunchtimes sitting beside the Thames, deep in discussion about the things he was learning. As he progressed with his studies we spent more time together and he became my first boyfriend. We went to see the new film 'South Pacific' and he dedicated the song 'Younger than Springtime' to me. On one lovely warm summer's day he took me to Reigate to meet his parents and then we had a wonderful picnic on Box Hill. I can still remember wearing my pink gingham dress trimmed with broderie anglais and a golden belt!

At about this time there were two conflicting British youth subcultures – the Mods and the Rockers. The Rockers rode motorbikes and their appearance reflected that. The Mods rode scooters and wore more clean-cut clothing. Someone proposed that a scooter could be a practical form of transport for Mum as, even then, she was having problems with her mobility. That was a very misguided and dangerous suggestion. She bought a pale blue Vesta scooter with disastrous consequences; her legs just weren't strong enough to support the weight of the bike and she was lucky to survive. We knew that a car would be the only practical option so we both applied for provisional driving licences and started taking lessons with the Dunstonian School of

Motoring in Petts Wood. Mum's instructor was Mr. Phillips, an ex-policeman with a bushy red beard. He told Mum that she would probably need one lesson for every year of her life and that worked out to be exactly true. Mr. Wadley was my driving instructor and I was the first to pass the test – albeit on my third attempt. We both learnt to drive in a Hillman Minx car, so when we eventually passed our tests, that was our obvious choice. Dad bought our shiny black 1957 Hillman Minx (registration number 504 KMG) from Dunstonian Garage for just over £400 and, although he couldn't drive at that time, he was very proud of his car and kept it in pristine condition.

In the summer of 1961 there was a series of international conventions and we were very privileged to attend the one held in Turin, Italy. Once again we travelled to Paris where we changed stations and, since we had time to spare, we hired a beautiful old Citroen taxi to take us on a tour of the city and a visit to Montmartre and the basilica de le Sacré-Cœur.

We then travelled overnight on the Orient Express across the snowcapped mountains of France and Switzerland and through the Simplon Tunnel to Milan, where we had to change trains to get to Turin.

Because Dad and I worked for British Railways we were able to enjoy free international travel – but only on certain trains. Unfortunately we were directed to the wrong train in Milan and we found ourselves travelling to Turin on the Rapido, which was a very modern, state of the art, high speed train. It certainly was an experience – a very fast but a very costly one!

The assembly was held at the site of the Expo 61 exhibition and, together with all the other visiting delegates, we stayed in the specially built halls of residence. We travelled back and forth to our accommodation on special buses where we had the opportunity to meet so many other wonderful brothers and sisters. One brother we met on the bus was George Koulouris from Greece. I rather fancied him although he was ten years older than me. We kept in touch and later he invited us to Athens for the international assembly that was planned for 1963. More about that later!

Attending the assembly in Turin was an amazing experience as the Italian brothers and sisters were so warm and hospitable. There were two lovely friends from Naples, Genaro and Enza, who took us under their wing and really looked after us. Back in 1961 there were only about 6,000 witnesses in Italy (now there are well over 250,000) and most of them managed to come to Turin for the assembly even though some were from the more impoverished areas of the country. One sister we met was called Concetta and although she had a large family and was very poor she had travelled up from Reggio Calabria in the south of Italy, just a stone's throw from Sicily. She also kept in touch with us as did many other of the young people we met.

In the picture below, taken at the assembly, there are from left to right: Giovanni from Pescara, Marilyn, Enza, me, Genaro, Mum and two sisters whose names I can't remember.

It was a six day assembly and we didn't want it to end as it was such a wonderful and faith strengthening experience. We spent the following week in Diano Marina, a seaside resort in Liguria. It was just a few miles south of Turin on the north-west coast of Italy, not far from the border with France.

Rodney, the young man from my office, was very nice, kind and well-mannered but he was rather intense and wanted a more serious relationship. He was also rather possessive. On one occasion I was aware that he had followed Ann and me to our weekly session at Streatham ice rink. I spotted him lurking in the shadows spying on us and I did something very foolish and immature. I wanted to teach him a lesson so I flirted with Spud, a big hunky member of the local ice hockey team and spent the rest of the evening skating with him. Spud was a powerful skater and with his strong arm around my waist I could skate like a professional. It was exhilarating, hurtling around the rink at breakneck speed! Rodney was very jealous and it made me realise that I was far too young and immature for any sort of relationship; the words of that popular song of the time were so true in our situation –

'She was only sixteen, only sixteen - but I loved her so.
But she was too young to fall in love - and I was too young to know.'

It became difficult working in the same office, so when an opportunity arose for promotion I successfully applied for a job as a draughtswoman in the Parliamentary and Survey section at the main offices in Waterloo Station. My work involved creating 'book plans' which were kept in the Houses of Parliament. (The railways at that time were operated by the government).

My job was to update plans that ran the whole length of each railway line continuously from one end to the other and were joined together in a concertina fashion. For example one plan would map the whole length of the track from London to Brighton with information about the ownership of all the adjoining land in case it should be required for compulsory purchase. Because these ownership details would constantly change, I was told that I had a job for life! For some that might have been good news but for me the idea of spending my entire life drawing miles of parallel lines with just the occasional distraction of a station or junction seemed an incredibly daunting prospect!

Although situated in the main building of Waterloo Station, our office was on one of the upper floors and looked out over the dirty glass roof. Instead of being able to watch all the interesting comings and goings and the hustle and bustle of the station below, all we could observe was the grey skies and the mating habits of the pigeons.

On one occasion the Chief Civil Engineer wanted his sixteen year old daughter to have work experience during her school holidays and asked me to give her some training in technical drawing. It seemed a nice thing to do but I didn't realise what a big responsibility it would prove to be. She was a pleasant enough girl from a very expensive private school but her artistic skills were nonexistent. Working in ink we used very specialised and expensive pens. Unfortunately, every time she attempted to draw a simple line she managed to break a nib and I was not popular with the man in charge of the stationery cupboard! During lunch time she wanted to go shopping in Oxford Street and that was also a bit of a nightmare. She was very naïve and I was petrified of losing her in one of the big London department stores; I knew she wouldn't be able to find her way back to the office by herself on the underground. It was a relief when her work experience finished and it was time for her to return to school.

There were some hunky young surveyors in our office who were part of Southern Region's rugby team. When a match was arranged with the team from the Eastern Region, they asked me to be their mascot to cheer them on. I went with Mr. Coleman, a clerical assistant from the office, and, since it was during working hours, it seemed to be a good idea at the time. I had never been to a rugby match before – and would never want to go again. The weather was terrible. We stood beside the pitch in freezing rain and I don't think I had ever experienced such biting cold. The match seemed to go on forever and I can't even remember which team won but at least we all had tea in the nice warm club house afterwards.

It was a nice friendly old fashoned office but the work, although highly paid, was very boring. I was stuck in a stuffy, smoke-filled room, drawing mile upon mile of straight parallel lines with nothing to break the monotony but the occasional station. I often thought of my friends, Ruth and Pam Adams; I envied them outside in the fresh air and sunshine, enjoying their pioneer ministry. They would never be materially rich but they were happy and had many spiritual blessings. After careful consideration I decided to hand in my notice and join the pioneer ranks.

I bought an evening paper to check the availability of part time employment and something rather strange happened. I was on the train travelling home when a strange little man, who was often in the same carriage as me, asked me if I was looking for a new job – as he would like me to work for him. I explained that I was only looking for part time work as I wanted to prepare to be a missionary – possibly in the Amazonian jungles!

"Well then," he said, "Don't worry about getting a job. Let me sponsor you and I will give you all the money you need to achieve your ambition!" I thanked him for his kind offer but explained that it didn't really work like that!

Dad wasn't too pleased about me leaving my job as he had hopes of me achieving a very high profile career on the railways but it turned out to be the best decision I have ever made. I honestly think the next few years as a Pioneer were the best years of my life. I was young, fit and fancy free and we had such fun and met so many interesting people in the field service.

Pioneering, at that time, meant spending 100 hours a month in the ministry as well as working part time to support myself. The ideal job would have been something for which I was qualified - but part time drawing office work seemed to be non existent. As a last resort I applied for a job as a mother's help with the Rutters, a wealthy family who lived in a large house in Petts Wood. Although I didn't mind looking after their young son, the domestic cleaning work that was also involved wasn't really my cup of tea and I didn't last very long!

The next job wasn't that much better. It was at the Curtis shoe shop in Cotmandene Crescent. I loved serving the customers but that job also involved cleaning and, since the other assistant was having an affair with the manager, I was always given the more unpleasant menial tasks which I didn't enjoy.

But then, suddenly and just at the right time, my prayers were answered! I saw an advertisement for work as a freelance draughtswoman/tracer. Although it meant acquiring a drawing board and all the equipment, it was an ideal opportunity. I could work from home whenever it suited me so it was perfect for rainy days. The drawings I did were interesting and varied and much of the work was marked 'Top Secret'. One week I could be working on plans for the new VC10 aircraft for Vickers Armstrong and the following week it could be for a gold mine in Africa. I picked up the plans from a small office in Orpington and was paid by the hour. I worked in my bedroom to the sounds of Radio Caroline or one of the other pirate radio stations of the time so I was very familiar with the latest pop music of the era.

Although I enjoyed my drawing work, the Christian ministry was of far greater importance and, together with my pioneer partners, Ruth and Pam Adams, Flo Baxter, Sharon O'Neil, Susan Whittlesea and later, my sister Marilyn, we shared some wonderful experiences. Sometimes we would meet up with some of the young brothers from Orpington Congregation and spend a day working in the countryside. Usually we would take our bicycles and work around our own estate or St Mary Cray village, which was also in our territory.

When Marilyn passed her driving test in 1962 she bought 'Speedy Gonzales' and that added a new dimension to our pioneering. He was a 1938 Austin 10, registration number COU 42 and cost £5. (If I had known my future married name would be 'COURT' I would have wanted to keep that number plate!)

Because we lived at the top of a hill and in order to conserve fuel (which at the time cost 4 shillings and 10 pence a gallon (less than 25 pence in today's money, which equates to under 5 pence a litre.) we could do many of our regular calls without even turning on the engine. From our house we would freewheel down Beddington Road to leave the magazines with Mr Bailey at the bottom. We would need a bit of a push to get to our calls in Whitewebbs but then cruised easily down St Paul's Wood Hill (where we picked up speed) to the bottom of Midfield Way to see Mr Coppard.

We met some very interesting people in the ministry. One unlikely elderly couple were the Darabs who lived in a spooky gothic house in St Mary Cray. He was a tall Persian professor and she was a short, plump English lady with dyed red hair who had served as an ambulance driver during the war. A teenage Persian boy, Farzad, lived with them and was training to be a ballet dancer.

They had spent a lot of time in the royal court of the Shah of Persia (Iran as it is now called) who was a close friend. Mrs Darab had actually written a book, 'The Shah and Persia' under her maiden name of Lois Gregory Khan.

Gholam Hossein Darab Khan, to give him his full name, had translated the works of Makhzanol Asrār, who was a famous 12th-century Persian romantic poet. He gave me a copy of his book 'The Treasury of Mysteries' – but when I opened it I was horrified to find a giant spider squashed between the pages! If only I had kept that book it would be worth a fortune as it is now very rare and valuable. The National Trust has a copy in the museum at Sissinghurst Castle.

"You can't possibly go in that old thing!" Mr. Darab had said when we told him that we were planning to go on a European adventure in Speedy Gonzales. "You are welcome to borrow my car instead." We were totally shocked – he was old, almost blind and we had absolutely no idea that he owned a car. He led us through the house into the back garden where there was a brick built garage. Throwing open the doors he revealed the largest and most beautiful car we had ever seen. It was a huge Daimler limousine, probably dating back to the 30's; the type that would have been used by royalty. It was in immaculate condition and when he pressed the starter, it purred instantly into life. We couldn't believe our eyes.

"It hasn't been out for years – you're very welcome to borrow it" he insisted. We looked at each other in total disbelief. There was no way we could take responsibility for driving such a magnificent machine but also there was the practical aspect – instead of miles to the gallon this would drink gallons to the mile, so we wouldn't have got very far on our limited budget. Reluctantly we graciously declined his very generous offer!

Sometime later Lois died and Mr.Darab asked me if I would like some of her shoes. He opened a cupboard and there was row upon row of the most amazing, extremely beautiful, jewel encrusted shoes. The Darabs must have had an incredible lifestyle in their heyday and she was obviously the Imelda Marcos of her time! Again I had to decline as the shoes were tiny; at least three sizes too small for me. I hope they ended up in a museum as each one was a true work of art.

I could write pages about all the interesting people we met but I will concentrate on just a few. At the opposite extreme there was Richanda who was a true Romany gypsy; a seller of sprigs of 'lucky heather'. She was very keen to learn about the Bible but I had to teach her to read before we could study seriously.

Then there was Nobby, who I thought was a very likeable young man. He was a bit of a joker with a great sense of humour.
"I'm Nobby. I'm a burglar!" he declared when I took him to the Kingdom Hall for the first time and introduced him to the congregation. Everyone laughed, but when I called at his prefab the following week it was all boarded up and the neighbours told me that he was in fact a notorious crook who had been arrested and sent to prison.

Shirley Beckwith was a lovely young girl whose father ran a bookbinding business in his garage. Shirley was doing well with her study so I invited her along to our Tuesday book study which was held in the home of Maud Dale, the only anointed sister in our congregation. We were all sitting round in a circle and Ken Thorne, our group study conductor, was just about to start. Suddenly Shirley, without any warning, fell forward into the middle of the room. She was having a very violent epileptic fit and nobody knew what to do. It was terrifying and seemed to go on forever but eventually she came round and was none the worse for the experience.

I also studied with Mrs. Keller in Marling's Park. She was a very aristocratic lady with royal blood who had escaped from Eastern Europe during the war and had some very interesting tales to tell!

I loved to accompany Mum when she studied with a lovely lady who lived in a very modern, architecturally designed house at the top of St Paul's Wood Hill. She was Beryl Gray, a well-known model and actress. Although she was incredibly attractive and had such a beautiful rich voice she was a very spiritual and modest person who loved the Bible and is still faithfully serving Jehovah today, more than fifty years later. So, as you can see, my ministry work was far from boring and I had the privilege of meeting some amazing people.

There were several eligible young men in our congregation. Michael Hastings was tall, gaunt and spotty and rode a rather decrepit looking motorbike. One day he offered me a lift and we ended up doing a ton (100 mph) down the bypass – one of the scariest moments of my life as I was only wearing a thin summer dress and no crash helmet (which weren't compulsory in those days). George Booker was tall dark and handsome and I went out with him for a while. He worked as a groundsman and was the heartthrob of all the local schoolgirls! He didn't drive at the time so we were often chauffeured by Tony Emery in his very large and ancient car (seen in the back ground of this picture taken outside Orpington Kingdom Hall).

There was one brother I did want to meet and I needed a crafty scheme to make it possible. Whenever I was out with Ruth Adams she was always on the lookout for a certain television repair man whose van was often in the area. She said he was a brother from Orpington congregation and lived at home with his mum. She seemed quite keen so I decided I had better check him out too. My brazen plan (not very discreet) was to go to his house on the pretext of doing calls in the area and ask if I could use the loo – and it worked! His mum opened the door, asked me in and introduced me to her son, David Court.

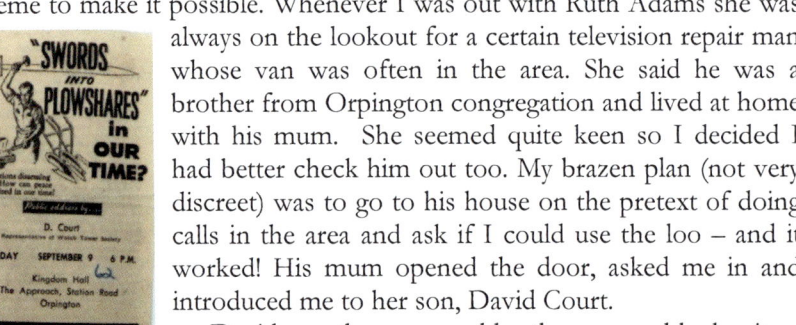

David was three years older than me and had quite a few responsibilities in the congregation. He was a pioneer and gave public talks. We started going out together but his mum was not too keen. She didn't like my green nail varnish or my aspirations to have an Alsatian dog and a Jaguar car. She definitely thought I was a bit weird and totally unsuitable for her son. David was quite a serious person and eventually agreed with his mum that I was far too zany. He decided to move away and was assigned to serve as a pioneer in Reigate congregation. That was an ironic coincidence because, although they didn't know me, I had acquired a terrible reputation in Reigate, which was Rodney's home town. After I stopped going out with him, Rodney left the truth and turned apostate – causing quite a lot of trouble for the local brothers. They obviously held me responsible for their 'Rodney problems'.

In 1963, a large group of Jehovah's Witnesses (mostly from America) embarked on a ten-week trip that would take them around the world. They were not typical tourists; their primary purpose was to find up-building Christian association at the series of "Everlasting Good News" Assemblies. Because delegates traveled to meet with Witnesses in over 20 countries, this series of conventions was dubbed the "Around the World" Assembly.

A highlight of each assembly was the talk entitled "When God Is King over All the Earth." Nathan Knorr, from the world headquarters of Jehovah's Witnesses, gave this talk at most of the assemblies. He described the world's worsening conditions and contrasted them with the Bible's grand promise of a restoration of Paradise to the earth. Worldwide, the combined attendance for this talk was 580,509.

The assemblies began in Milwaukee, Wisconsin, U.S.A. From there, the delegates traveled eastward. After the New York assembly, they stopped in England, Sweden, Germany, and Italy. At each location, they found opportunities to share the good news spoken of in the Bible. They then moved on to Athens, Lebanon, Jordan, Israel, and Cyprus. The final leg of the journey took them through Asia and the Pacific to India, Burma (now Myanmar), Thailand, Hong Kong, Singapore, the Philippines, Indonesia, Australia, Taiwan, Japan, New Zealand, Fiji, and Korea. The trip drew to a close in early September with assemblies in Hawaii and California.

Here in England, our assembly was held at Twickenham Rugby ground and because we lived comparatively locally we were involved in much of the preparatory work. In advance of the assembly we shared in the 'rooming' work. This entailed calling at homes in the neighbourhood to find reasonably priced accommodation for the visiting delegates. If the householder offered a spare room we would have to make sure it was up to standard.

The assembly was to last for eight days and the sessions were in the afternoon and evening. In the morning the delegates had the opportunity of going in field service or enjoying sightseeing trips to places such as

Stonehenge, Windsor Castle and Hampton Court. One of the most interesting tours was to the British Museum – and I was chosen to be trained as a guide for that trip.

Ken Harrington, from our congregation, was a London cabbie and as such, had an intimate knowledge of the city. Most weekends we went up to the museum in his taxi to be taught about all the amazing exhibits that were relevant to Bible history. This Bible tour included most of the notable and useful artefacts in the British Museum that would assist with our personal study, faith and ministry. It explored the links between the pagan practices of the Egyptians and the religious rites of Christendom today! We also learnt about the origins of language and writing and saw some truly amazing examples in the form of tablets and carvings that strengthened our faith in the Bible's historical and prophetic records. It was a real privilege to be part of this work and I was able to share my knowledge whenever I visited the museum for years to come.

The assembly itself was amazing. There is a very interesting contemporary news video about all the different aspects of the assembly on this website: www.britishpathe.com/video/witnesses-baptised. It describes how the grounds around the stadium were turned into a little town with large marquees complete with beds, washing facilities and food preparation. In those days all our meals were prepared on site and served on metal trays in large dining tents. Each day at least 30,000 meals were served! It was all very highly organised and the food was wholesome and delicious. There were over 800 baptised and so many people at the stadium for the public talk that the stands were filled to capacity and overflowed onto the grass of the playing field.

Rather than travel up each day, Mum, Marilyn and Christine stayed in the marquees but I camped with my friends at a special theocratic site near Shepperton. We had a wonderful time and wanted it to go on forever.

As mentioned earlier, one of the assemblies was scheduled for Athens. I had kept in touch with George Koulouris, the brother from Greece who we had met two years earlier in Turin. I was longing to meet him again and this was the perfect opportunity. Marilyn and I booked a package holiday with Olympic airways; it was our first flight and our first trip abroad without our parents so it was all very exciting

When we arrived in Athens we discovered that the assembly had been cancelled because of pressure from local religious leaders although we were still able to meet up with the delegates and participate in the many sightseeing tours that had been arranged. However, my main reason for going to Greece was to meet up again with George.

Athens 1963

He had sent me a photograph in which he appeared to look like a Greek god – and that was how I always pictured him. When we actually met, I realised that photo was about 15 years out of date! Nevertheless George was a lovely person and he and his family were very hospitable. George lived in a small single storied house in Nikea Piraeus which was a suburb of Athens. He lived with his parents, his sister Esther, brother Demetrius and I think there were other brothers also. The house was very primitive with only two rooms and an outside hole in the ground toilet. We were staying in a modest hotel in Athens but we enjoyed many meals with the family. It was our first encounter with rustic Greek food which usually included egg plants as they called them, drenched in copious amounts of olive oil.

George met up with us every day and took us to see all the important sights of Athens: the Acropolis, the Parthenon and the Areopagus (where the apostle Paul made his famous speech). He took us on a boat trip to the Temple of Poseidon on the island of Sounion – (famous for its sunsets), to a lovely sandy beach where we swam in the Aegean Sea, and up into a forested area of the mountains where it was refreshingly cool after the oppressive August heat of the city.

Temple of Poseidon at Cape Sounion
1963

At the end of our holiday we waved a tearful goodbye to George at the airport – but then there was a problem with the plane and it seemed that we were going nowhere. Olympic Airways was owned by the multi-millionaire, Aristotle Onassis, and he arranged for us to go for a wonderful lunch at one of his seafront restaurants (his yacht was moored in the bay outside) and then we were taken for a scenic coach tour along the beautiful Aegean coast. After a night in a luxury hotel we finally boarded the plane for the return flight home. Although I had once hoped that there might have been a glimmer of romance - nothing came of it and I heard George went on to be a well-loved circuit overseer.

Marilyn and I both had pen friends who lived in the South of France and went to a boarding school in Valence d'Agen, a little town in the department of Tarn-et-Garonne. My pen friend was called Solange Yon and Marilyn's was Nicole Selle. I never got to meet Solange but in 1964 we were invited to stay with Nicole's family who lived on a farm at Le Campsas,  a very rural part of Southern France. We were still pioneering and didn't have much money but planned to go on an exciting camping trip, driving through France to Spain and then visiting Marilyn's pen friend on the way back. At the time Marilyn was working at the Oil Well, a petrol station near Swanley and occasionally, when they were short staffed, I also helped out there.

I particularly enjoyed helping out over the Christmas holidays as we earned lots of tips! We met some very interesting characters at the Oil Well. There were the charming Spanish waiters with their impressive cars - Manuel had a Jaguar and Louis had a Ford Capri. They worked at The Bull restaurant next door to the garage and once took us out for a meal at a posh London restaurant. Then there were the firemen from Swanley fire station with their fire engine and many other unusual or eccentric regular customers – all of whom we recorded on one of our old cine films.

One of the firemen took a fancy to Speedy Gonzales and Marilyn decided to upgrade to a more reliable beige Austin Somerset (GRD 735) 'Gertie', which cost £85 from Alfie Beard's garage just down the road from the Oil Well. She sold 'Speedy' to the fireman for £5 and, much to our surprise, discovered later that he was actually a brother from Orpington congregation - when we saw the car parked outside the Kingdom Hall!

Despite Mr. Darab's kind offer to lend us his beautiful Daimler limousine, we thought Gertie would be more suitable for our European adventure! We loaded her up with all our camping gear and set off with high hopes, but things didn't go exactly as planned when we had a puncture soon after we got off the ferry. It was really early in the morning, and we had to wait on the forecourt of a little village garage until a very helpful local stopped to help! That evening we found a lovely little camping site and as we were attempting to put up the tent (it was our first experience of camping) we couldn't find the tent poles. Our hearts sank with the realisation that we must have forgotten to pack them. We took everything out of the car and, much to our relief, discovered them hidden away on a ledge right at the back of the boot!

It was lovely driving through the French countryside. There wasn't much traffic and we stopped occasionally by the side of the straight tree lined roads to open the bonnet to let the engine cool down and have a little picnic; heating up cans of peas, soups and various delicacies on our little Calor gas stove.

On the third evening we were pitched at a lovely campsite beside the beach at the foot of the Pyrenees. There was a violent storm in the middle of the night and the tent blew down. From then on we decided give up on camping and stay in more solid accommodation.

We had a couple more punctures but our biggest problem was the starter motor which had a tendency to jam. On one occasion we were on the railway level crossing at Cerbère. The car stalled and the starter jammed and we were stuck on the main Paris to Barcelona railway line. We couldn't move and we could hear a train coming in the distance. Fortunately there was a rubbish lorry behind us and all the dustmen came and pushed us off the track, averting a possible disaster! I have been terrified of level crossings ever since!

On another occasion we were driving along an elevated coastal road with a sheer drop down to the sea far below, when we noticed that we were being followed by a police car which eventually pulled us over. We weren't aware that we had done anything wrong so, when the two officers approached, I decided to pre-empt the situation by winding down the window, smiling sweetly and asking them if they had any scissors as I had broken my finger nail! They went back to their car and returned with a first aid kit. Finding some nail clippers, one of them proceeded to gently trim my nail and then waved us on our way. I still don't know what that was all about!

1964

1964

After a few days exploring the South of France, including a trip to Spain, we made our way to Le Campsas to visit Nicole, Marilyn's pen friend. They lived in a beautiful rambling farmhouse deep in the French countryside between Montauban and Toulouse. The Selles were a lovely family with ten children and they were very hospitable. Water had to be pumped from a well and food was cooked in a large cauldron over an open fire. When we left they gave us a wonderful picnic to eat on the way home, including a roasted chicken and a large box of the biggest peaches I have ever seen.

The farm is now a famous winery, the Château Boujac, run by Nicole's brother Phillippe and his wife, Michelle. Their wines are produced from Négrette, one of the rarest varieties of black grape which is exclusive to the area. They have a website: www.chateauboujac.com.

On the way home we stayed in the Grand Hotel, Toulouse – by accident rather than design, as it was the only accommodation we could find. It was the poshest hotel I had ever been in – it even had a telephone!

When we arrived in Paris we had great fun, driving up and down the Champs Elysees and round and round the Arc de Triomphe - trying out each of the 7 lanes in each direction. As a passenger it was quite scary but Marilyn seemed to enjoy it!

It was at the 1964 'Fruitage of the Spirit' district assembly at Twickenham that I spotted my former boyfriend, David Court, sitting with Bert and Mary Bowtle in the opposite stand. He was wearing sunglasses and I thought he looked rather like my heartthrob, Omar Sharif! We met up, resumed our friendship and started going out together again. By this time I was older and wiser and he had come back from Reigate to live with his Mum in Orpington. By the end of the year we were engaged and planned to marry the following October. We bought my beautiful antique diamond engagement ring in a pawnshop in Croydon.

1965

The convention in the summer of 1965 was 'The Word of Truth' assembly held in Scotland at Murrayfield Stadium, Edinburgh. It was a long way to travel and I think special trains were provided for the brothers. We loaded up the Hillman and took the car on the motorail service (which stopped running years ago). This was much easier than driving all the way as we had planned a tour of the Scottish Highlands after the assembly. David returned to Orpington but our family stayed on to explore the beautiful Scottish castles, lochs and mountains.

Edinburgh 1965

When we got back we had to start preparing for the wedding. Mum made my wedding dress and I borrowed the veil from Ann, one of my Romany Bible studies. Ruby, David's mum, made the cake and organised the catering. She was a brilliant cook and discovered that she had a remarkable talent as a wedding organiser. Together with her trusty team of helpers she went on to cater for many more weddings, each larger and more elaborate than the previous one! The nearest licenced Kingdom hall was at West Wickham (Kent) so we had to arrange that, and book Farnborough village hall for the reception. Marilyn was my bridesmaid, Dad gave me away and Bert Bowtle conducted the service. David's best man was Ken Barlow who he had stayed with while pioneering in Reigate.

Finding somewhere affordable to live after the wedding was proving to be more difficult. Most of the flats that had been advertised were already taken by the time we applied or else were totally unsuitable. Mr. Darab, my Persian friend (mentioned earlier) was quite keen for us to rent a flat on the top floor of his large gothic house. His wife, Lois, had recently died and the house felt strange and rather spooky. He led us up the dark, creaky staircase and showed us into the flat, which obviously hadn't been occupied for years. The first room we entered was huge and empty, except for a large cobweb covered Victorian roll-top bath in the middle of the room; nothing else – just the bath. The rest of the flat was no better and we knew it wasn't for us! The wedding was fast approaching and we still had nowhere to live. I decided that our only hope was to get up early on the day the local paper was published, go to the Kentish Times factory and try to get a copy hot from the press. I remember sitting in the car outside the offices, scanning the advertisements, hoping to be the first to apply for anything suitable.

I spotted something that did seem ideal: 'Furnished studio flat above the stables of a country house - £6 per week'. Although it was still early, I went to the nearest phone box to try to make an appointment. The lady sounded rather posh and it was obvious that she would be very particular about choosing potential tenants.

She agreed that I could go round straight away and she gave me the address and directions. She was Mrs. Knox-Johnston, the mother of round-the-world yachtsman, Robin Knox-Johnston. The house was a large country mansion called The Rookery, just outside the village of Downe in Kent. The beautiful building dated from 1724 and had connections with Kew Gardens. Charles Darwin, who had also had lived in the village, used to observe specimen trees in the four acre grounds and wild orchids from all over the world, which were planted in the greenhouses.

The Stable Flat at The Rookery, Downe

The flat was above the brick and flint built stable block which was being used as a garage. There was a flight of stone steps leading up to the front door on the side of the building. This opened into a small vestibule with a bathroom to the left and a kitchen on the right. Ahead was a very large fully furnished room with beams and a window overlooking the gardens. The furniture was old and rather shabby but comfortable. There was a skylight in the ceiling which would be perfect above my drawing board – I was still doing my freelance drawings at the time.

It was obvious that she was rather 'upper crust' and would expect her prospective tenants be of similar standing. I knew it was important to make a good impression so I drove up in Dad's shiny Hillman Minx and when asked what David did for a living, I replied in my most refined voice, "Oh, he's 'in television!'". That did it – we were in! It must have been a bit of a shock when we turned up after the wedding in a battered old radio and television repair van complete with tin cans and 'just married' stuck all over it!

2nd October 1965

2nd Oct. 1965

The wedding went well and we had a lovely day with our respective families and our friends from both congregations. Back then it was the custom for those who couldn't make it to send greetings telegrams which were read out at the reception. We even had one telegram from the congregation in Reggio Calabria, right down in the southernmost tip of Italy!

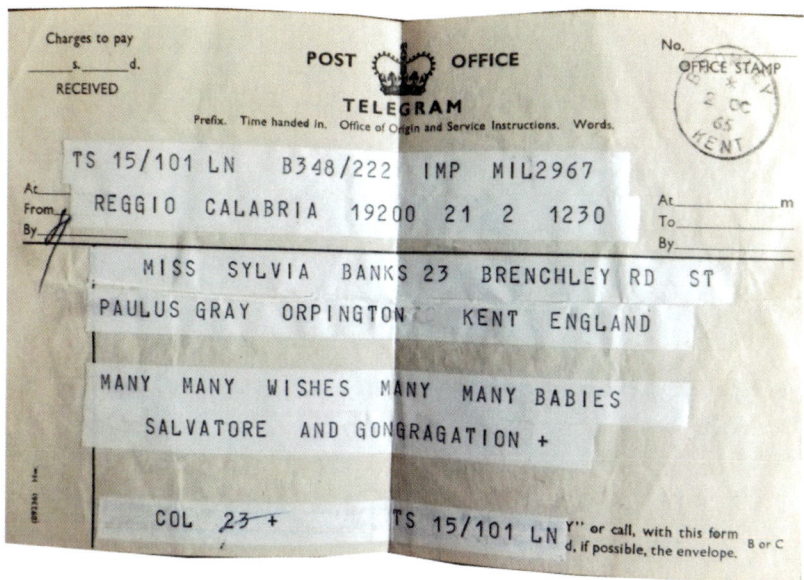

David and I were married for 51 wonderful years until he passed away peacefully on the 7th December 2016 at the age of 77. A detailed and illustrated account of the time we spent together can be found in the book I wrote after his death, which is available on Amazon both as a paperback and an e-book; David: The Life and Times of David Henry Court.

At this point in this book I have covered 100 pages and have only just reached the age of 22, so I won't bore you any more with my life story as it is comprehensively covered in David's book – designed as a companion and counterpart to this one! So, that's it – apart from two more brief but important chapters to conclude this volume.

CHAPTER 7
FINDING CHUCK
2012

"I've found him!" my sister, Marilyn, cried, excitement rising in her voice. "But not only that – he actually wants to meet us!"

With trembling hands and mixed emotions I replaced the receiver. At the age of almost seventy, the eldest of three sisters from an ordinary working class family background, the realisation dawned that I actually had a brother, a complete stranger about whom we knew nothing.

It all began a few years ago when I innocently began to research our family history. With the advent of so many helpful genealogical websites it wasn't too difficult to delve into the past, especially as my mother's maiden name was quite unusual. However, when searching the records to confirm the birth dates of various family members, I discovered something that didn't quite tie up with facts I already knew. A baby boy, who had been named David John, with the same surname as my mother, had been born in August 1932.

Out of curiosity, my sister, Marilyn, decided to send off for a copy of that birth certificate. It came as quite a shock to discover that David's mother was in fact our mother too. It was even more of a surprise to discover that the place of birth, when I checked it out, was actually a workhouse.

Mum had often spoken of her happy childhood in Chelsea, where her father, until his tragic death when she was ten, was butler to Sir Robert Burnett and her mother was head cook in the household. After leaving school she worked as a milliner in Mayfair and then in 1940 she married my Dad, but we knew nothing about what had happened in those intervening years.

David, if he was still alive, would be over eighty. What sort of life had he experienced? Did he know about us and would he want us to find him? Marilyn was determined to find out. She trawled through phone books and searched all the available records but it was as if David had never existed. Maybe he had died or perhaps he had changed his name. If so, we had little chance of ever finding him. Marilyn, however, was not about to give up.

Our only hope was the possibility that Mum, who had died over ten years previously, had secretly kept some information that would give us a clue. Without much expectation my younger sister, Chris, began sifting through a box of old documents that she had found in the loft. Much to her surprise, she discovered an envelope containing three photographs. There was one photo of a small baby in a pram, another of Marilyn and me with an older boy, taken in our garden soon after we had moved into our new council house in 1950, and another, more recent photo, of a young couple with an Alsatian dog.

Examining those photographs, things slowly began to slide into place. I didn't recognise the baby in the pram but I vaguely remembered the photo being taken in the garden when I was about seven. Mum had prepared a special tea for a visitor who had been introduced as David, a young man who, we were told, worked with Dad. He was nice and we talked about horses, which were a passion of mine at the time, but I don't remember much else about his visit. Marilyn and Chris thought they recognized the later photograph which was taken about 1966. They had gone with Mum on a nostalgic visit to Gloucestershire to revisit Mr. Whitman's house in Driffield where we had been evacuated during the war and the quaint Cotswold stone cottage in nearby Daglinworth, where Mum had spent some childhood holidays with her grandmother. Apparently they had also called in to see some of Mum's 'old friends', Chuck and Yvonne, who lived in a caravan on Leckhampton Hill, near Cheltenham. They were sure these were the people with the dog in the more recent photograph. Although I didn't go on that visit, I do remember it for a good reason. It was soon after our wedding and house prices in Kent were far too expensive for us, so we were looking elsewhere and asked Mum to bring back a newspaper from that area so we could check out the local values - which ultimately resulted in us buying a little house in Stroud.

Since Mum had kept the three photos hidden together, it seemed likely that they were linked in some way – and possibly to her secret past involving David. Was it conceivable that he might have changed his name to 'Chuck' and, if so, what was his surname? The detective work continued and Chris found one of Mum's old address books. Among the more familiar names of family and friends there was just one entry that we didn't recognise – 'C & Y Kemsley', with the address of a quarantine kennels near Gatwick Airport. Could 'C & Y' be Chuck and Yvonne? There was a dog in the photo with Chuck and Yvonne; dogs were obviously in the kennels, so could 'dogs' be the missing link?

As expected, the Kemsleys were long gone from the kennels but at least we had a possible name to go on. With nothing to lose, Marilyn typed 'Kemsley; into a search engine and up popped 'Charles Kemsley – dog trainer' complete with address and telephone number! Without hesitation she dialled the number and the man who answered assured her that he was indeed Chuck Kemsley and confirmed his date of birth (which was the only definite thing we knew). Amazingly she had found our long lost brother!

I felt concerned about how he would feel, meeting up with three complete strangers claiming to be his sisters! I needn't have worried. Although frail and bed-bound, we found Chuck bright as a button with a cheeky grin and a wicked sense of humour. He looked so much like my Mum. She had suffered from a rare genetic disorder, which Chuck had also inherited. This rendered him almost immobile but, like her, his brain was certainly not affected.

There was so much we wanted to ask him, but didn't want to tire him out. He talked a bit about his colourful past and told us he was actually in the process of writing his life story. However, when I plucked up courage to ask what he knew about his early life, his expression changed.

He explained that from an early age he had been told that he had been found abandoned on the doorstep of 40, Brunswick Square in London. This sense of betrayal and rejection had obviously affected him deeply. He had been fostered until he was five and then sent to a very harshly disciplined, pro-military type prep school. While there, one of the teachers falsely and maliciously told him that the reason his natural parents had dumped him was so they could go off and enjoy themselves without any responsibility. Feeling bitter and traumatised by this revelation, he grew up with a chip on his shoulder and a volatile temper. It was as though he had a death wish, living from one dangerous experience to another.

I couldn't believe that Mum would abandon a baby on a doorstep as she was a woman of great integrity and high moral values. I knew that, however desperate her circumstances, she would never have ever considered doing such a terrible thing. I needed to find out more and the first thing I did, when I got home, was to google that doorstep address that he had given us: 40, Brunswick Square. To my surprise I discovered that it is now the address of the Foundling Museum, formally the Foundling Hospital, in London. They have a very comprehensive website and, with Chuck's permission, I was able to make contact with Val, a very helpful senior social worker within the organization. Amazingly, even though it was so long ago, she was able to look up complete records of everything that had happened at the time; the circumstances of his birth, the name of his father and even statements from my mother's family, friends and employers.

As opposed to all the lies Chuck had been told, we found out that my mother had done her very best to try to keep him. Apparently, as a naïve and vulnerable young woman, she had been seduced and then dumped by an older man when she became pregnant. She took him to court to apply for an Affiliation Order but, to her devastation, he denied responsibility and the case was dismissed on the grounds of insufficient corroborative evidence. With no home of her own, no prospect of marriage, and no income other than what she herself could earn, she must have felt that she had no choice but to make the hard decision to part with him. She applied to the Foundling Hospital for advice and the committee of Governors accepted that she had lived an honest and hardworking life (one of their requirements). They then assured her that it would be in the best interest of the child if he were taken into their care. By this time Mum had cared for the baby for three months and it must have been very difficult and heartbreaking for her to part with him. It was, however, a sacrifice she felt she had to make to ensure his future care and well-being.

It was their practice in those days to change the children's names to protect the confidentiality of both mothers and babies, and to give them the opportunity of a fresh start in life. On the very day of his admission into the Foundling Hospital's care, he was baptised and given the new name 'Charles Kemsley'. At that time, the governors did not allow mothers any further contact with their babies, and they were not encouraged to make enquiries about them. Despite that, however, Mum regularly wrote many letters over the years, seeking news and showing concern for his wellbeing. Every birthday and Christmas she included a special gift or a sum of money, which was deposited in a savings account in his name. Unfortunately Chuck was completely unaware of this. He only ever received one of the presents, a tennis racquet, but was only allowed to play with it for two hours before it was taken away. He knew nothing about the many other gifts or the money.

It must have come as quite a shock when, eighty years later, Val, the lady from the Foundling Museum, went to meet him in person. She told him about everything that had really happened and the circumstances of his birth. She reassured him that his birth mother had never forgotten him and that he was constantly on her mind throughout his childhood. She actually gave him a cheque for the money that had been put into his savings account all those years ago. Even more importantly she presented him with the many original letters that Mum had written enquiring about his welfare. It was amazing that those letters, together with copies of all the identical, impersonal, and curt replies assuring her that he was well - even when he wasn't, were still in existence. Seeing those fragile handwritten letters must have been quite an emotional experience for Chuck who had gone through life believing that he had been abandoned and that nobody cared about him.

At the outset I said that I had mixed emotions when Marilyn began her search to find Chuck. I was so afraid that if she succeeded it would all end in tears. However, instead of the disaster I dreaded, it has been an amazing experience that has resulted in so many blessings for us all.

Chuck had discovered the real truth about his birth instead of the lies that he had been told throughout his childhood. He now knew that he had a devoted mother who always kept him in her heart but was prepared to make the ultimate sacrifice in order to give him a better chance in life and opportunities for the future that she was unable to provide.

We had the privilege of getting to know a charming man who has lived life to the full. True to his word, he sent us every chapter of his life story as he wrote it – and what an amazing story it is. They say that truth is stranger than fiction and this really is the case with Chuck's book.

He was a man who lived life on the edge, seeking out danger and defying death at every opportunity. He travelled the world; fearless, tough and invincible until he met Yvonne, his true love and soulmate, and together they discovered a unique talent that made him one of the greatest animal trainers of our time.

Not only does his story describe the incredible and amusing events that happened throughout his life but it also reveals the unique methods by which he successfully trained thousands of dogs, together with their grateful owners.

Chuck died in 2015 and I had the honour of officiating at his funeral at Medway Crematorium on the 4th July 2015. My next project will be to consolidate all the information I have, both from the Foundling Museum and from Chuck himself, and attempt to write a book that will do justice to his incredible life story.

It will be called 'Finding Chuck!'

CHAPTER 8
IN CONCLUSION

David's death made me appreciate just how precious and fragile life is and how suddenly and abruptly it can be cut short. In my own case I feel so privileged that I am still here; that I have actually passed my sell-by date of three score years and ten - despite three major and potentially fatal health issues and several other life threatening situations when a split second either way could have made the difference between life and death.

David was just an ordinary man, but for those who knew him, he was a very special person. He was a kind, gentle, conscientious and spiritual man; a loving father and a wonderful husband. I wrote the book 'David' in his memory, not just for therapy for me at a difficult time but because I wanted people to know about him and what he accomplished in his life. I could write with confidence about the time we were together but the rest could only be gleaned from information people told me. His father had been killed in the war, leaving his mother devastated and traumatised. I wish I had known more about those dark days of his childhood and the difficult teenage years that followed. For that reason I am writing this book about my own life now, while I still have the ability and capacity to remember what happened and how I felt during my early years.

Like David, I am not rich or famous; I have always been hopeless at sports; I can't sing and, despite my best efforts, I have never been a successful cook. However, throughout my life I have always loved animals, natural history, travel and the arts. People have said that I am creative and I suppose that is true. From an early age I loved to paint and draw. Later, in the 1980's, I became interested in ceramics and sculpture and then, when I retired in the 1990's, I bought a camera and enjoyed photography.

I never had the pony, Alsatian dog or the Jaguar car that I desired in my youth but I did get my dream cottage. From a very early age I used to draw pictures of a little double fronted thatched house in the heart of the countryside, surrounded by pretty flowers and lots of animals. That dream became a reality when we bought Tythecott Cottage. At the time it was a dilapidated hovel but over the years and with a lot of hard work, we transformed it to a beautiful chocolate box cottage. We lived there with a succession of wonderful pets for almost half our married life. Because of its isolation, our cottage was the ideal location to host an annual congregation garden party which became known as the 'Tythecott Festival'. Many people still remember those wonderful summer evenings with so much talent on display - music, singing, dancing, poetry, comedy sketches, Bible dramas, acrobatics and even performing dogs. After the show there was dancing in the moonlight with the local band and hot dogs were served from the barbecue which, on one occasion, almost set fire to the roof!

David, Jessie and me outside Tythecott Cottage 1999.

The nearest I got to owning a pony was this rocking horse which I recently restored. However, during our marriage we did have many pets including geese, chickens, rabbits, a goat, budgerigars, fish, at least eight Siamese cats, not counting their kittens, one zany Springer Spaniel, Lucy, and two very intelligent Border Collies – both called Jessie.

Our latest dog is a 'Poppypoo' called Sparky. His mum is Poppy and his dad was a miniature poodle. Poppy is a pretty little dog who looks a bit like a fox. She was rescued from Ireland and came with many issues, but now she is much better and they get on well together.

Full details of all our various pets (including the saga of Rodney the goose) are recorded in the 'David' book- as are most of the other interesting events that happened during our married life. However there are just a few significant things which I will include in this volume.

As mentioned earlier, I do enjoy travel and had several continental adventures before I was married. David however wasn't very keen and it took until 1989 before he ventured on his first trip abroad. Of all the warm Mediterranean holiday destinations he could have chosen, David decided that the only place he wanted to go to was Russia - in the middle of winter!

He actually found it so interesting and exciting that after that there was no stopping him! We travelled all over Europe, cruised down the full length of the Nile in Egypt and watched the opera in the magnificent Roman Arena in Verona, Italy. However, the most memorable trip we had was in December 1999 when we arranged to take a group of fellow Witnesses on a Bible tour of the Holy Land. It was an amazing experience which really brought the Bible to life. We sailed on the Sea of Galilee, crawled through Hezekiah's tunnel, walked in the foothills of Mount Hermon, floated in the Dead Sea and stood on the Mount of Olives overlooking Jerusalem and the Temple Mount. We even met up with the brothers from the Bethel in Tel Aviv and visited the Kingdom Hall in Haifa to meet the local congregation. It was the real trip of a lifetime!

Our group of Witnesses on the Mount of Olives, overlooking Jerusalem and the Dome of the Rock which was built on the site of the Temple.

Another significant event happened in 2005 when we bought a villa in Fuerteventura, the second largest of the Canary Islands in the Atlantic Ocean, just off the west coast of Africa. We had planned to live permanently on the island. David was an elder and could serve in the small English speaking congregation which, at that time, was meeting in the Kingdom Hall in Corralejo. Unfortunately his responsibilities in our local congregation in Bideford delayed the move and then ill health prevented it happening at all. Nevertheless we were able to make frequent trips to the island which has now been declared a biosphere reserve. I will always remember my first visit and the excitement I felt when I saw our private pool – something I had always wanted but never thought would ever be possible!

During our years at Tythecott Cottage I had a studio with a kiln and produced all sorts of pottery. At first I had a stall in Bideford Pannier Market but then we rented a shop called 'The Dragon's Lair' in Torrington Pannier Market. Although I made a wide range of various types of ceramics, dragons were very popular at the time and became my best selling pieces. My dragons were always very friendly ones and I became known as 'the dragon lady'! As well as pottery and ceramics we also sold a variety of other locally made arts and crafts, including jewellery, woodwork, candles, leatherwork, metalwork, corn dollies, paintings and many other interesting and unique creations.

For a short time I worked as a clerical assistant in the Benefits Department at Torridge District Council. It all started when they were overwhelmed with so much filing that they asked if I would come in for just one day to help out. That one day extended into the next and then the next and eventually I was offered a permanent job. When I retired a few years later I bought myself, as a leaving present, a simple digital camera. I had never really been interested in photography and certainly wouldn't have considered it to be a form of art. How wrong could I be! That evening we took the new camera down to the sea at Westward Ho! and I took my very first photographs. The sun was setting and a surfer was coming back up the slipway. I entered that photo in a competition and was amazed when, sometime later, it appeared on the front cover of the Sunday Times magazine!

My camera was a Fuji model and, back then, the company ran a monthly photographic competition. The theme for the March competition was 'Mad as a ....' We were in Fuerteventura at the time and I couldn't find anything 'mad' to shoot – so I decided to provide my own. I drew and cut out two cardboard hares, painted them black, mounted them on wooden skewers and stuck them in a rocky wall at the end of the road. I couldn't believe it when the resulting photograph won first prize in the competition! After that there was no stopping me – I entered every photo competition I could find even though I knew I would be competing against experienced and professional photographers. Despite the fact that I really knew nothing about photography, I became quite successful and won numerous prizes, awards

and even a medal.

Some of my prize winning photographs.

In 2014, David became seriously ill with acute ulcerative colitis and it seemed unlikely that he would survive. Against all the professional predictions, he made a remarkable recovery and was able to attend the international convention at Twickenham that summer and Suzie's graduation the following spring.

In October 2015 we celebrated our Golden Wedding anniversary with a wonderful afternoon tea party arranged by the girls, followed by a fantastic cruise on Cunard's Queen Victoria.

Sadly David passed away on 7th December 2016, but I am so grateful that together we have had such a wonderful and satisfying life and enjoyed so many marvelous blessings - the greatest of these being are our two beautiful daughters, Rebecca and Suzanna and our two charming grandsons, Elliot and Ben.

SYLVIA COURT

Printed in Poland
by Amazon Fulfillment
Poland Sp. z o.o., Wrocław